Tourette

That's What Makes Me Tic

Victor Mizelle

WestBow
PRESS
A DIVISION OF THOMAS NELSON

WestBow Press books may be ordered through booksellers or by contacting:

WestBow Press
A Division of Thomas Nelson
1663 Liberty Drive
Bloomington, IN 47403
www.westbowpress.com
1-(866) 928-1240

Because of the dynamic nature of the Internet, any Web addresses or links contained in this book may have changed since publication and may no longer be valid. The views expressed in this work are solely those of the author and do not necessarily reflect the views of the publisher, and the publisher hereby disclaims any responsibility for them.

Any people depicted in stock imagery provided by Thinkstock are models, and such images are being used for illustrative purposes only.

Certain stock imagery © Thinkstock.

ISBN: 978-1-4497-0690-6 (sc)
ISBN: 978-1-4497-0691-3 (e)

Library of Congress Control Number 2010939292

Printed in the United States of America

WestBow Press rev. date: 12/16/2010

THE ROCK-A-TEENS   ROULETTE RECORDS   GENERAL ARTISTS CORPORATION
NEW YORK CHICAGO BEVERLY HILLS DALLAS MIAMI BEACH LONDON

INTRODUCTION

In 1885 Gilles de la Tourette, a French physician and neurologist, formally described a syndrome he had observed in nine patients at the Salpetriére Hospital in Paris. In fact, the symptoms had been known, and described in previous writings, dating back to 1489. But it was Tourette who clearly defined the complex tics involved, and suggested that they merited recognition as a distinct syndrome. American psychiatry officially "recognized" and codified this entity in 1980, by addition to its manual of disorders, the DSM III. In the current edition (DSM-IV TR) it resides among "tic disorders," in the section called "Disorders First Evident in Childhood." But it is a lifelong affliction; there are several helpful medications, cognitive and behavioral interventions, and some promising new treatments including deep brain stimulation. There are also many patients whose symptoms persist despite these options. The eminent neurologist and writer, Oliver Sacks, has given a wonderful account of a gentleman in Western Canada with severe tics, who is nonetheless a fine surgeon and a skilled private airplane pilot. Tourette patients vary in the severity of their symptoms, and for each patient, tics may "wax and wane" over time. Several prominent historical figures are believed to have had symptoms consistent with Tourette's, and many contemporary writers, athletes, and performers have identified themselves as Tourette patients.

It has been my privilege to be Mr. Mizelle's doctor, intermittently, for some 16 years, and I was honored when he asked me to write this introduction. During this time, of course, our primary focus has been on defining and trying to alleviate the challenging symptoms of Tourette Disorder. These included a diverse, unusual, and oft-changing array of sudden motor tics (grabbing at his nose, repetitive sniffling, stomping one foot); and problematic vocalizations. Inevitably, though, the symptoms became part of Mr. Mizelle's life story, and of coping with the problems they caused him. I learned of his disrupted childhood, his difficulties at school, his stigmatization by peers. He told me about his five marriages, undermined by his illness, but with hope persisting for intimacy and love. I met his fifth wife, and heard of both her frustrations and admiration. I learned of their enduring friendship, even after separating. We talked about his jobs, his strong work ethic, and the inability of employers to tolerate his tics.

And, remarkably, there was his music. Mr. Mizelle found, in the guitar and singing, a voice that was clear, pleasing, and tic-free. From his teens, he became involved in country music, and the newly emerging rock and roll. He really was there at the beginning—for Bill Haley, Elvis, and Buddy Holly. When he was 24, he and his band mates wrote a hit song ("Woo Hoo"), which in 1959 earned them a place on the Dick Clark Show. The fate of that song, and its ownership, became another setback in Mr. Mizelle's life, one that may finally be righted in his senior years. His love for music, and performing, never wavered; in country bars,

Moose Clubs, and VFW Halls, he kept on playing, his body relaxed and his lyrics smooth, as long as the guitar was in his hands.

Imagine an illness so quirky that it causes one to do or say the very things he would most like to avoid. It is an experience of mass compulsions—a steady buildup of inner tension that becomes almost unbearable, and is temporarily relieved by a jerking movement, a grunt, or a shocking set of words. Like other Tourette patients, Mr. Mizelle often compares these urges to a sneeze: a rising state of discomfort whose discharge provides relief, but may be awkward and alienating.

I know Mr. Mizelle well, not just as a patient, but as a human being. He is a kind man, and a tolerant one; decades of coping have probably made him so. He harbors no prejudices, is not a racist, sexist, or chauvinist. Yet his relentless disorder compels him to say terrible things, often the most offensive thing possible in a given situation. For many reasons, he must use the city buses in Richmond, most of whose riders are African American. What would be the worst thing for a solitary white man to shout in such a setting? The awful "N-word," of course. And the pressure to utter this epithet builds within Mr. Mizelle at every bus stop. Sometimes he can clench his jaw and suppress the word into a mumble; sometimes it bursts forth in an explosive yelp. Inevitably, he has been confronted, but how to "explain oneself out of" a behavior like this? (We talked about his carrying a card, or even a sign, that quickly explains the symptoms of Tourette, but would deeply offended people believe such a thing?) Riding an elevator, he may find himself suddenly accompanied by women. Now the "P-word" comes to the fore, and a struggle to reach his floor before he embarrasses everyone. At dinners with his wife, he would praise her cooking, try to use good manners, but could not suppress the nasal snorts that disgusted her.

Like many people with a chronic childhood illness, Mr. Mizelle's life story involved growing up with enormous challenges—lost freedoms, time missed from school, separation from peers. But the unusual, and then poorly recognized symptoms of Tourette's, greatly compounded young Victor's difficulties. His sudden impulses to strike himself in the groin, or to bark out loud, did not evoke sympathy or caring from teachers or counselors. His behaviors were misunderstood as deliberate provocations by a hostile and uncivilized boy, and so the burdens of social stigma and rejection were added to his lot. His account of an ostracized and perplexed youth trying to survive in the social order is understated and poignant.

Mr. Mizelle's life with Tourette's also, remarkably, provides a kind of history of twentieth-century American psychiatry. The many treatments which he was offered (or to which he was subjected) reflected psychiatry's changing currents. At 6 Victor began striking his groin and using profanity; soon afterward, he started barking like a dog. His first physician, the family GP, prescribed a circumcision and tonsillectomy. Not surprisingly, the symptoms continued; as he got into conflicts with teachers and school authorities, he faced beatings from his father and grandmother.

At age 12, he was brought to the Medical College of Virginia for an evaluation; it was noted that his motor tics and vocalizations were triggered by the presence of other people. A year later, he was hospitalized at a private facility, Tucker Psychiatric Hospital, where three psychiatrists were involved in his care; he received Dilantin (an anticonvulsant drug), Phenobarbital (a sedative and anticonvulsant), cold body packs, and a course of electroconvulsive therapy (ECT). When funds ran out, he was transferred to Eastern State

Hospital where, at age 14, he was the youngest person on the "receiving ward." He endured threats and abuse by other patients, but did get the luxury of an observation period, without treatment. A psychologist took an interest in Victor, and began sessions of psychoanalysis 5 times per week; he never learned his diagnosis, and had no sense of benefit from the sessions. He remained at Eastern State for nearly four years. At 17, he was sent to Johns Hopkins Hospital, where he spent two years, and his "treatments" included insulin sub-coma, and even an exorcism! Plans were made to give him a prefrontal lobotomy; thankfully his parents refused consent, and spared him permanent injury. After attempting and failing to function back at his parents' home, he returned to Eastern State Hospital, and remained there until age 21. He resumed psychoanalysis, again without benefit. The staff offered to hospitalize him for life as a "public nuisance," but his parents again intervened and took him home. He had spent nine years in psychiatric facilities, received little formal education, felt socially incapable, and retained many tics. He did receive music lessons, a bright spot that helped sustain him.

In 1965 a psychiatrist/psychologist couple, Doctors Arthur and Elaine Shapiro, began using the medication haloperidol in successfully treating some Tourette Disorder patients, and described their results three years later in the British Journal of Psychiatry. Their work challenged the prevailing view that this was a purely psychological disorder, and also led to the founding of the Tourette Syndrome Association. Additional dopamine-blocking drugs were later applied, followed by modest results from still other classes of medication: Clonidine (an alpha antagonist), buspirone, SSRI antidepressants, SNRI's, etc.

Understandably, given his frustrating years of confinement in the 1940's and 1950's, Mr. Mizelle was not eager to seek out psychiatrists as these new developments emerged; experience had made him wary and skeptical. In 1975, his former psychoanalyst wrote to him about the emerging awareness of Tourette Disorder, and of successful treatments with haloperidol. Five years later, he did attempt an outpatient medication trial; unfortunately he got only uncomfortable side effects, and no benefits. In 1994, a mutual acquaintance of ours, who had played in bands with Mr. Mizelle, suggested he come and talk to me. We reviewed all that he had been through, and the modern treatments now available. Over the years, we have tried a range of dopamine blockers, antidepressants, anti-anxiety medications, and behavioral techniques, with modest and often transient results. We have also discussed the newer neurosurgical approaches. Mr. Mizelle continues to do what he has done for seven decades: cope as best he can, find solace in music and friends, and allow his resilient personality to transcend his symptoms.

John R. Urbach, M.D.

FOREWORD

Tourette Syndrome is a neurological disease, somewhat like Parkinson's disease. One difference is that Parkinson's produces no vocal tics, but it does have some of what are called *motor tics*. As far as I know (not being a doctor, just a victim) there is no known cure for Tourette. Also called the Orphans' Disease, it produces vocal and motor tics. The motor tics are sudden jerks of the body; for example, when sitting down, the Tourette victim bangs his elbows against whatever is available at the time. It also produces skipping or stomping of the feet when walking. It is almost impossible to run at any pace, as the person will surely fall. There is also banging of the head, twisting of the nose (causing it to bleed), and hitting oneself very hard in the genital area. As for vocal tics, Tourette causes profanity, barking like a dog, or racial slurs. These are called *coprolaleia*. The person has no control whatsoever over his or her tics, and it can be pure hell every day.

Tourette is a very rare disease. It was discovered by an 18th century neurologist named Giles Tourette, and the disease bears his name. Not all Tourette victims have the same tics. Some just have vocal and some have both, and the duration of the tics is not very long but they are very constant. There are some medications that will relieve certain tics to some extent, such as Haldol, a dopamine blocker. It has been said that people with Tourette syndrome have too much dopamine, unlike Parkinson's patients who have too little.

Tourette victims are usually socially unacceptable, meaning that the profanity can become severe. People with Tourette can and do get into a lot of trouble. Some, like myself, have been threatened and have had to fight to protect themselves. For some victims, the only peace they get is when they are asleep.

Tourette is hereditary, and the symptoms usually don't show up until around six or seven years of age. I am using myself as an example. I have been a victim for over 70 years, with no relief. It is a very depressing disease for which there is no known cure. It's almost like a curse.

It was thought for years to be a mental disease, and only recently has it been recognized as a neurological disease. It has been estimated that only about a million or so have Tourette, but that is only a guess and may not be the case at all.

Parents of young Tourette victims sometimes get on a guilt trip and blame themselves or God. There is no explanation or reason for it, and only God knows the cause and cure. Being a victim myself, I can really sympathize with anyone suffering with the disease. I have often been on a pity trip, feeling sorrow for my "thorn in the flesh," crying and blaming God for my mishap—but to no avail. I have been beaten and reprimanded by my own father, and spent all of my teenage years in mental hospitals. I have been misdiagnosed, and told that I could be incarcerated for life, just like a criminal. But God has spared me that.

Well, that's all I know about Tourette, and I am no expert on the subject. My heart goes out to all victims of this terrible and misunderstood disease. We live one day at a time, and pray that science will find a cure.

My name is Victor Mizelle. I have a disease called Tourette. The symptoms of my disability began in my early childhood, but let me start at the very beginning. I was born Clarence Mizelle. I was named after my father whose middle name was Clarence. I was also born with the malady—it is hereditary. I had no symptoms until about 1940, when I was six years old.

I was born at home in September, 1934, in Norfolk, Virginia. I don't recall much of my life before I was six years old. I do remember that my parents argued and drank a lot, and I recall my father abusing my mother and sometimes even hitting her. Even at my early age I tried to protect her, but to no avail. I was not an obedient child and I was a bit cantankerous. I vividly recall being in a flood when I was only two or three years old. We were living in Ohio in a town called Mingo Junction. It was right on the Ohio River, which floods almost every year. We were on the third floor and the water was almost up to the window. We had to climb out of the window to get into a boat that was already overloaded. I don't recall how long we lived in Ohio. We must have moved from Norfolk to Ohio but I don't know why. Anyway, I believe that somehow we ended up back in Norfolk—my memory is very vague. I do recall that we moved in with my aunt, my dad's sister.

Almost all of my father's family lived in Norfolk. My father was the oldest of four brothers and one sister. Some of my uncles on my father's side were musically inclined; most of my mother's family were tone deaf.

I hate to say this, but my father was not a good provider. He was a house painter. Oh, he played music professionally, but he could not support a family playing music, and he soon gave it up. My mother worked from job to job, and we moved in with relative after relative.

I believe I do remember some tics before I was six but, again, my memory is very vague, and I don't recall what they were or how severe they were. I never attended kindergarten, but I do recall attending a school—I believe it was in Norfolk. I think I was four or five years old but, again, there is a lapse of memory. As I remember, I was in a talent show at school, and I was supposed to sing a song. I was terribly nervous, but I did my best—I recall some type of tic, like movement. (I'm not sure if it was vocal or motor.) My choice was a song called *Amapola, My Pretty Little Poppy*. I don't know where I learned it. I believe Gene Autry had a recording of it in the early 1940's and it was a hit record for him. Anyway, I got halfway through the song and I wet my pants. Well, I didn't finish the song, and I ran off the stage crying and embarrassed. That was the end of my singing career for a while.

After living from relative to relative in Norfolk, I believe we moved to Portsmouth, Virginia. I think my father had gotten a job at a shipyard either in Portsmouth or somewhere in the surrounding area, and my mother had landed a job at the American Tobacco Company. I don't know why we moved to Portsmouth, because the American Tobacco

Company is in Richmond, Virginia, and it's a hundred-mile drive from Portsmouth to Richmond. I think we had a car but I'm not certain. But I am sure of her job because she would bring home free cigarettes, and that's when I began smoking. I was severely punished for it.

Anyway, we moved into a housing project called Williams Court. The rent was very cheap, about $60 per month. We had two bedrooms, a living room, a kitchen and a bathroom. The house was heated by a coal stove, and the coal bin was on the front porch. 148 Magazine Road was my new address; it was our first house. That's when my Tourette tics became really apparent.

I remember my first tic. I began hitting myself very hard in the area of my genitals. Also, I started barking like a dog. Even at that early age, I realized there was something wrong with me, but I did not have a clue as to what it was.

I tried putting my hands in my pockets, but the tics were so violent that I tore the bottoms from my pockets. Later I began using profanity. I don't really know where I learned foul language. I suspect that I learned this from my father who was used to cursing.

Soon after my initial cursing outbursts, I began taking the Lord's name in vain. I thought for sure He would strike me with a bolt of lightning. (We were not a religious family. We did have a Bible, but it was seldom read to me. I remember my father as being sort of religious. I believe my grandfather was a minister, and he may have added this dimension to our extended family.)

I began attending a local school in Portsmouth. We lived in a small housing project close to the school. Because of my tics, I did poorly in school. I was either sent to the principal's office, sent home, or the teacher would make me stand in a corner. Sometimes my isolation lasted for an hour or more. Academically and behaviorally, my report card was terrible. My father would take a belt to me, thinking this would change things.

My father was a house painter, but he was unable to get steady work. My mother and father would go to what was then called a beer garden, and drink. My dad was a part-time professional musician. In fact, he was playing a gig the night I was born.

To entertain himself and his friends, he would play the guitar and sing to pass the time at the local bar. Sometimes they would take me with them, and I would stand up on a table and sing. I could sing the popular songs like *Coming In On A Wing And A Prayer, When Johnny Comes Marching Home,* and *Boogie Woogie Bugle Boy* by the Andrews Sisters. My tics did not bother me when I was singing, but afterward they would come back stronger than ever.

In school, my tics continued to be a problem for me and for my teachers. Before the 5th grade, I was removed from public school. My teacher suggested to my parents that they should seek medical help for my problem. Apparently, because I was hitting myself in my genitals, the medical treatment deemed appropriate was for me to be circumcised.

Tourette Syndrome was never mentioned after I was removed from public school. I was seen by many doctors, but Tourette Syndrome was never mentioned. I was having a very difficult time with my tics. I did not make friends very well, and the friends that I managed to have were not very good for me. They made fun of me and laughed at me. Sometimes I would have to fight to protect myself.

About 1945 my mother, my father and I moved from Portsmouth to Hopewell, Virginia. My parents split up, and my mother and I went to live with my maternal grandmother. Hopewell is a small town about 20 miles south of Richmond.

In spite of my tics, my mother decided to enroll me once again in public school, which was across the street from my grandmother's house. I started in the 5th grade, but I did no better there than in the schools I previously attended.

My grandmother was not very understanding of my tics. She told my mother in no uncertain terms that she thought I could control them, and that I was doing them deliberately. There were often hard feelings between my mother and my grandmother. My mom was always on my side. When my mom wasn't there, my grandmother would spank me because I said such dirty words. It got so bad that my mother and I left my grandmother's house and moved to the west end of town. Mom rented a two-bedroom house, and my grandfather (my mother's father) moved in with us.

Soon after we were settled, my father also moved in with us. He begged my mother for this reconciliation and promised to be a loving husband. We did not know where he had been while we were at my grandmother's, but (because of me) my mother took him back.

My mom was traveling back and forth from Hopewell to Richmond to work. She worked at the American Tobacco Company in Richmond, and my father worked when he could. I no longer attended school. I stopped at the 5th grade.

We all got along very well. My grandfather was deaf, so my tics didn't bother him. My father began to understand that I couldn't control the tics and outbursts.

I had two uncles (my mother's brothers) who would visit us occasionally on weekends. I hated to see them come, because everyone but my mother would get drunk. My two uncles would offer me money if I would do my tics. Then they would bet on how long I would go without saying dirty words or barking like a dog.

Sometimes my Mom would get drunk, too. In spite of their being drunk, both Mom and Dad would take up for me against my uncles. An argument—sometimes a fist fight—would break out. I would run into my room crying. After everyone became sober, the matter was forgotten. My mother and father soon tired of the hassle and told my uncles not to visit any more.

Because I wasn't attending school, I got a part-time job at a service station. I was about 11 years old. My tics prevented me from doing many things that other children were doing at the same age. Many of the children that I knew were going to movies or riding bicycles. The only time I seemed to be at peace was when I was sleeping.

At least I had my job. One day, the owner of the service station and I went into town for some auto parts. I was told to stay in the car. I got bored sitting there alone and decided to open the glove compartment. There was a gun inside.

I knew nothing about guns, but I took the gun out and started to play with it as though it was a toy cowboy gun or a water pistol. It did not occur to me that I was playing with a real gun that might be loaded and dangerous.

The gun had a clip that was used to hold the bullets. I managed to pull out the clip and saw that it was empty. What I did not know was that there was one bullet in the chamber. I thought I was having fun, but I was being quite stupid. I was looking down the barrel and pulling the trigger. The safety was on, and the gun did not fire. Surely God was looking out for me!

During my play shooting, I clicked the safety off. I pointed the gun barrel against the palm of my left hand and pulled the trigger. I remember hearing a very loud bang, and when I looked, I had blown a big hole in the middle of my hand. There was a lot of pain, even though my hand felt completely numb.

Even now, I can't describe the amount of pain I felt. My hand was swelling up, and there was blood—*my* blood!—everywhere. The bullet went through my hand and through the left door. We never found the bullet.

It took me a bit of time to realize exactly what had happened. If the safety had been off when I had the gun to my eye and was looking down the barrel, it would have been all over. I believe it was an act of God that spared me. Finally I jumped out of the car and ran into the auto parts store. The owner met me as I was running through the store.

"What the hell happened?" he hollered. I did not have to explain, for when he saw my bleeding, swollen hand he said, "We have to get you to the hospital." In the short time from the accident until I stood inside the store, my hand had swollen to twice its size and was bleeding badly. It took some time to reach the hospital, and my tics were out of control.

"Calm down," the owner shouted. "We'll be there soon."

When we arrived at the hospital I was immediately rushed into the emergency room. I was doing tics like crazy. The doctor cut away the damaged skin to reveal a large hole through the palm of my left hand. After cutting away all of the damaged skin, he poured almost a whole bottle of alcohol onto the wound. I let out a yell that I am sure all in the emergency room could hear. I jumped off the table and began running around and doing lots of tics. The doctor got me back on the table and stitched the open wound in my hand. I don't recall how many stitches were sewn to close the wound, but it was a lot.

Meanwhile the owner had gone to get my father. He could not phone, because we did not have a telephone. My parents could not afford the monthly payments.

The doctor put my arm in a sling, and the owner drove us home. Somehow my mother knew what had happened, for she ran from the house to greet us. She said, "My poor baby, are you all right?"

I wanted to curse and yell, "No! I'm not all right. I'm hurting!" and curse some more, but I held back and said, "Yes, Mom. I'll be all right."

We lived in Hopewell until about 1948. Because my mother wanted to be closer to her job at the cigarette factory, we moved to Richmond, Virginia. My father got a job at Philip Morris, too. We moved into a one-bedroom apartment with a kitchen. It was small but comfortable. I slept on a cot in the kitchen. The bathroom was a community bath located in the hallway.

I tried a different school again. It was a special school for children with problems, but that did not last long. The tics were dominating my life, and it was like living in hell.

I saw a few doctors at the Medical College of Virginia. They suggested that I should be hospitalized. They believed that I had a nervous condition called *Saint Vitus' Dance*. Once again, Tourette Syndrome was not mentioned. I was never diagnosed with the disease during my childhood.

It is surprising to me that no medical professional who had observed my behavior seemed to suspect that I had Tourette Syndrome. The condition was known since the 18th century. It was discovered by Giles Tourette, and the condition bears his name. There are many medical books about Tourette Syndrome. It is a genetic disease that seems to have been described hundreds of years ago. To date, there is no known cure.

But that is another story. As I said, I was never diagnosed with the disease in my early life. In early 1948 several doctors requested that I be admitted to a sanatorium called Tucker's. I was only thirteen years old, and all I ever knew was hospitals and doctors. My parents were reluctant to put me in another hospital, but they had run out of options. My malady was socially unacceptable, and I could not function very well in society. I was poked and jabbed.

I received different kinds of medications but nothing did any good. I would curse the doctors and nurses, and I was very different from the other patients. I could not control myself and would call the nurses dirty names. I would make sexual advances toward the nurses.

After all these medications and treatments failed, they put me on EST—electric shock treatments. On the morning of my treatment I could not have any breakfast because I would vomit during the treatment. I had no idea what was happening to me. I was taken to a simple room where there was a stretcher. I was restrained with leather belts and buckles. One doctor administered the treatment, and three or four nurses held me down. I was terrified. The doctor applied some type of salve or gel to my temples and two electrodes were attached. I would hear a loud buzzing noise and then become unconscious. There was no pain. They took me back to my room after the treatment.

When I woke up I had a throbbing headache. I don't know how long I was out. Also they had me restrained to my bed. I couldn't walk for a while. The nurses would check in on me from time to time. They would give me water, because I was always very thirsty after my treatment. I felt like I had been to hell and back. My tics were no better. For a while I received a shock treatment every other day. I had nine or ten of them in a row.

I dreaded these treatments. After they discovered that the shock treatments did no good, they put me on another treatment called "cold packs." I was taken to the same room where I had the electric shock treatments. They put me on a stretcher and wrapped me in wet sheets. They poured buckets of ice over the sheets until I was completely covered.

They restrained me to the stretcher, and I was left alone for hours at a time. It felt like I was freezing to death.

The nurses seldom checked on me. I had a difficult time being iced down. I continued to tic. I had vocal tics as well as motor tics. I don't have a clue as to how many cold packs I had, but it did not help relieve my symptoms.

My parents came to visit me as often as they could. On one of these visits they said they were concerned that I was not any better. My father was very angry. He confronted my doctors and asked them what the problem was. They had no explanation as to what was wrong with me. Again, there was no mention of Tourette Syndrome.

I really don't know how long I was at Tucker's. Eventually my parents could no longer afford the cost, whatever it was. My doctor suggested that I be admitted to a state hospital for evaluation. The closest one was about 50 miles from Richmond in Williamsburg, Virginia. Again my parents were reluctant, but they finally agreed.

On August 19, 1949, my parents took me to Eastern State Hospital in Williamsburg. They drove me there in their car. There were no toll roads or interstate roads then; they took Route 60 East going 50 miles per hour. We stopped to eat, so it took a little longer than two hours to get there.

On the way my parents and I discussed my condition. Some of the way, my dad and I would sing together. He would sing lead and I would sing tenor harmony. I must have inherited my musical ability from my dad, because my mother couldn't even play the spoons!

When we arrived in Williamsburg we found the hospital easily, because Williamsburg was a small town. Eastern State Hospital was really old; it was built in the 18th century. I was admitted at the receiving office. My mother couldn't stop crying. Even my dad shed a few tears. Before it was over, all three of us were crying together.

After being admitted I hugged my parents and kissed them goodbye. They said they would come to visit me as often as they could. After bunches of hugs and kisses, an attendant escorted me to my room on the first floor. Later I found out it was called "The Snake Pit."

I entered the room, and the heavy wooden door was shut and locked. I looked out the window and watched my parents drive away. I already missed my mom and dad, and the worst part was wondering if I would ever see them again. I began to cry heavily.

After a while I stopped crying. They did unlock my door, and I decided to explore the floor. I walked down a long hallway where there seemed to be many rooms where other patients lived. One room had long wooden tables where patients were sitting. Some were just walking around mumbling to themselves. Some were fully dressed and some did not have all their clothes on.

The smell of urine was overwhelming. I felt like I was in prison. Later I found out that I was the youngest patient residing at the hospital. This made me a target for sexual harassment.

About lunchtime an attendant came and lined us up. He escorted us to the dining room, which was right across from the Snake Pit. While I was in line I yelled a verbal tic.

The patient behind me cursed and angrily asked, "What is your problem?" I thought he was going to physically attack me. I told him that it was just a nervous condition. He responded, "Why don't you take some *#*#* medication for it?" I didn't have much of an answer, so I tried to muffle my tics. He seemed to back off after this.

I finally reached the steam tables. The menu was hot dogs and beans. I piled my metal plate with franks and beans, and I also got a cup of coffee. The food had no seasoning at all, and the coffee tasted terrible.

I found out from one of the other patients that the coffee tasted bad because the hospital staff put something called *saltpeter* in it. I had no idea what that was. I managed to eat the franks and beans, but I couldn't stand to drink the coffee. In fact I never drank the hospital coffee again.

I sat by myself most of the time, and I never really made any friends.

After lunch an attendant would escort us back to the Snake Pit. There was nothing to do. Most of the residents would play cards or checkers. I recall that there was a TV set, but I can't be sure of that.

I began masturbating a lot when I was young. I seemed to have a very strong libido. I wasted most of the day in my room, walking around or looking at magazines. Everyone had to be in bed by nine o'clock. After roll call I would try to go to sleep. Many nights I cried until I finally fell asleep.

I would always have to watch out for older patients who tried to sneak into my room to try to attack me sexually. A few times they managed to get in. I told an attendant about it, but that was fruitless, so I just did the best I could. A lot of the sex offenders would stay away from me because of my tics. This was a blessing in disguise. I stayed away from everyone as much as possible.

I had not seen a doctor for some time after I arrived at the facility. One day, one of the many doctors left a message for me to come to his office in the administration building. That was where most of the doctors had an office. An attendant escorted me there; it was just a short walk. My tics were coming fast and furious. The attendant asked me what was wrong. My reply was that I didn't know, but I thought it was just a nervous condition. He warned me that some people might not understand and might try to harm me. I agreed with him, and he said no more about it.

When we reached the doctor's office the attendant knocked on the door. We heard someone call for us to come in. I went in, but the attendant stayed outside and turned to go to the canteen just down the hall.

When I stepped into the doctor's office, he was sitting behind his desk. He was writing some notes on a sheet of paper. I introduced myself—my name back then was Clarence William Mizelle. Later, when I became an adult, I changed it to Victor Mizelle.

He introduced himself as Doctor Davis. He was a gray-headed, elderly man, probably in his early sixties. He told me to sit down. He said that he wanted to ask me some questions about my nervous condition. He wanted to know how I was doing. I told him that I had had the condition most of my life. I said that the first recall I had was when I was about six years old. I told him about the different hospitals where I was admitted, about the treatments that I had received, and the different medications that were prescribed.

I began to cry and told him that my life had been a living hell. I wanted to know what was wrong with me. I said that when I was talking or otherwise preoccupied, I didn't seem to have tics.

Finally I stopped crying and apologized for breaking down. He assured me that the medical staff would try to help me. I told him that during childhood I had been diagnosed with St. Vitus' Dance Syndrome. He said that the diagnosis might be true, but that he couldn't be positive about that possibility. He told me that he would be my regular doctor, but that other doctors would be seeing me also. The visit lasted about an hour. After we were finished, I was escorted back to the Snake Pit.

I was on the Snake Pit for a long time, and I made the best of it. I had a lot of hassles from other patients. I was made fun of, poked, laughed at, and threatened a lot of times. As I have mentioned before, I stayed to myself a lot of the time. Most of what I did was eat, sleep, tic, and try to get along with the other patients.

After a long stay on the Snake Pit, I was transferred to the second floor. It was an open ward, and I got ground privileges. I could come and go as I pleased as long as I was back on the ward by the six o'clock whistle that blew from the power plant.

I had a lot of time on my hands with nothing to do, so I would take walks around the hospital grounds to get familiar with where everything was. I found the canteen and the recreation building. I also found the women's ward; it was called Covington. That part of the hospital was taboo, and was off limits to male patients. There were a lot of women walking around who also had ground privileges. Most of the patients with ground privileges spent their time at the canteen.

I made regular visits to the PX where things were really cheap. The jukebox there was a nickel, cokes and soft drinks were a dime, and—believe it or not—you could get saltpeter free in your coffee for a dime.

My favorite song on the juke box was Les Paul playing guitar and Mary Ford singing, "How High the Moon." I would play this song whenever I had a nickel to spare. Les Paul was a guitar player that I truly admired. He was my idol. Although I had never tried to play a guitar, he inspired me to learn how to play one.

Some days I had more control over my tics. At other times (truthfully, most of the time) I had no control whatsoever.

There were some fine-looking women who hung out at the canteen. I was always trying to get them alone, but because of my tics I didn't have much luck.

One day I talked one of the female patients into taking a walk with me. She asked me about my tics, and I explained to her that it was a nervous condition and that I couldn't help it. I wasn't a bad-looking guy at the age of fifteen. Her name was Dot; she was much older than I was, and she was very pretty. We ended up under the laundry building. It was my first sexual experience with a female. The whole experience lasted a short time. I did notice that there were no tics during that time.

It was quite hot under the laundry building. We actually met quite often, but she was furloughed, and that ended this activity for a while.

My favorite sport was—and still is—fishing. Sometimes I would go off the hospital grounds and search for a creek or river to fish. I would cut a wooden pole, tie a piece of string to the end, get a can of worms, and I was all set.

I took a big chance in leaving the hospital grounds. It was against the rules but I did it anyway. I was never caught. It felt good just to be alone. I could tic out of control, and it really didn't bother me very much. I just did not want to bother other people.

When I was off grounds, if I wasn't fishing I was looking for girls. I did get a part-time job in the hospital kitchen cooking powdered eggs, bacon, and brewing coffee laced with saltpeter.

The menu was different every day. One day it was hot dogs and pork and beans; the next day it was roast beef with powdered potatoes and no gravy. Friday was always fish day. I don't know what kind of fish—it had no seasoning at all. All vegetables were from a can.

My pay was very low—I got about a dollar a month. I guess the low pay was because the hospital had about twenty-five hundred patients. I didn't complain. At least I had a bed and the food was free.

There was a certain routine at the hospital. The patients with ground privileges could go and come as they wished, as long as they weren't late returning. Wards Five and Six would eat last. These wards were where the really dangerous patients were housed. The hospital never left them unsupervised; they had no freedom, and two or three attendants escorted them everywhere they went. When they got inside the dining hall, some of them would immediately run to the garbage can and begin to eat what was in it. The attendant would force them back to the food line. Sometimes the attendants would grab them around the neck and drag them to the food line.

I could not stand to watch this cruel treatment, and eventually I quit working in the kitchen. Nobody seemed to care what was happening. The behavior of the attendants was never reported. I was going to blow the whistle, but I was warned to keep my mouth shut if I knew what was good for me.

It was just as bad on the Snake Pit. While I was on the second floor, I observed patients from the Snake Pit going for a shock treatment on the fourth floor. Some of them were elderly men who did not want to go to the treatment. They would have to pass my floor. There were no elevators, and they would have to climb three flights of stairs to reach the fourth floor. An attendant would force the patients up the stairs, dragging them by the neck. Some patients were almost carried this way up the stairs. Some of them would be out cold and have to be revived prior to the treatment. I was upset by the cruel treatment, but I didn't say anything. This seemed to happen almost every other day.

Once I was sitting in the canteen drinking a cup of old coffee and listening to my favorite song, "How High the Moon" (I almost wore the record out!) when the attendants told me that my parents were waiting to see me. I was so glad at the thought of them visiting me that I ran to the receiving office where they were waiting. I hugged and kissed them several times. I hadn't seen them for almost six months. They had to rent a car, because their car was broken down, and they couldn't afford to come very often. My dad presented me with a brand new rod and reel. I was glad to see them together.

They asked me how I was doing, and I busted out crying. I told them that I wanted desperately to go home. They noted that my condition was no better than when I was admitted. They said that they would try to get me a furlough at Christmas time, but that was a long way off.

I told my dad that I was interested in playing the guitar. He said that he would try to get me one if he could find one that he could afford. He said that if he found a guitar for me he would bring it to me on his next visit.

During this visit, I asked my dad what saltpeter was used for. He laughed and began to explain the use for this item that could be purchased at any drug store. He said that it was used in prisons to keep the inmates from getting an erection. He said that it was sometimes used in the military. In a joking way, I told him that it might work on other people, but it sure did not work on me! We both had a big laugh and the matter was dropped.

My parents stayed for a couple of hours. I hugged and kissed them goodbye. They left, assuring me that they would visit me again whenever possible. I tried hard to hold back the tears, but I just could not keep myself from crying.

I did a lot of fishing with my new rod and reel. I never kept any of the fish I caught. They were mostly catfish, perch or carp. Sometimes if I caught a lot of fish, I would sell them to black families who lived along the way that I walked to go to the water. I didn't charge a lot. It was just a little extra spending money in my pocket.

Sure enough, on my parents' next visit, they brought me a shiny new guitar. I asked my dad how much it had cost.

He thought for a while and finally said that he had had just enough to buy it for me. He sat down and showed me how to form some chords. He would name them for me as he played them—A, B, C, D, E, F, and G, just like the first seven letters of the alphabet.

After they left I continued to play the chords just like he showed me. My dad had written me a chord chart. I practiced endlessly every day. I was getting pretty good, but I had a difficult time forming certain chords because of the gunshot wound that I received as a youngster. I could play most of the chords, but I could not play a C-chord or an F-chord. After a while I realized that I would never be as good as my idol, Les Paul.

I discovered something else that was very important to me: I did not usually tic when I was playing the guitar. I do remember one incident when the guitar did not save me from embarrassment. I was sitting outside on a bench playing my guitar when a fine looking nurse stopped to listen. I wanted to impress her with my talent, but for some reason—just because she was standing there—I yelled out a dirty four-letter word. That was a surprise, because I did not usually tic when I was playing. She began telling me in no uncertain terms that I should watch my mouth. I tried to explain to her that I couldn't help it, but she refused to listen to me. She just kept on bawling me out. I tried several times to apologize to her, but she refused to accept my apology. The conversation became so loud that one of the hospital doctors that happened to be passing by came to my rescue. He informed her that she was wrong in thinking that I was acting deliberately. She began to argue with him about the dirty word that I had used. He told her that this would not be the last time that she would hear that word, and that she should back off. She left like she was madder than a wet hen.

The doctor and I sat talking about my tics. He said that he was a psychologist; I didn't know what that was. He asked me if I would come to his office the next day. I agreed, and we parted company.

I hadn't seen my regular doctor for a while, and I wondered what this doctor would do for me. So every morning at 9 a.m. I met him at his office. It was in the same building as my regular doctor. I walked down a long hall of offices until I came to his office. On the door, in big black letters, it read **Doctor David Orr, Chief Psychoanalyst**. I knocked on the door and heard, "Come in."

He was sitting at his desk. A reel-to-reel tape recorder was on the desk in front of him. He looked like the spitting image of Jack Webb, of *Dragnet* fame. He had coal black hair and was very thin. I stared at him for a long time, and he invited me to sit down. I sat in a large leather chair. He asked if it was OK for him to record our conversation.

I said, "Sure, no problem."

He clicked on the tape recorder and began to ask me questions. He asked me to tell him everything I was thinking about. I thought this was a dumb way to proceed but I agreed anyway. He asked me about my childhood, and I told him as much as I could remember.

He asked me about my mother and father, and every time I would tell him about these incidents, he would say, "What do you think that all means?"

I told about my hospital stays and about the treatments I had received. I told him about the medications prescribed for me and that I did not have a choice about taking the medications.

He said that I had been through quite a bit. I agreed with him.

We discussed a lot of things. As in the past, I was not told that I had Tourette Syndrome. It was never mentioned to me until many years later. I never understood how the doctors at that time could be so ignorant of a malady that was hundreds, or even thousands, of years old.

The session lasted about an hour. He asked me if I wanted to come back at the same time next morning. I agreed to meet with him at that time.

It was still early when I finished my session, so I hung around the canteen for a while drinking coffee, playing the juke box, and (of course) seeking out female patients willing to take a walk with me. If I had no luck, I would practice on my new guitar, which I kept under my bed in my room.

During my stay at the hospital, I learned a lot of things that I could do. After my sessions with the doctor I would go to the pottery class and work with clay. I also learned to do needlework and knitting, like *knit one, purl two*.

My occupational therapist was a very beautiful lady. Her name was Miss or Mrs. Gilmore. (I didn't know if she was married or not.) I did hope I could get her alone. She had long blond hair and a beautiful figure. Every time I got the chance, when I sat down next to her, I would try to peek inside her blouse. I got away with it for a while but was finally caught in the peeking act. I could have been locked up on the Sixth Ward for such a dumb stunt! I just thank the Lord she did not report me.

So I had to say goodbye to OT services.

I continued my sessions with Doctor Orr, but nothing seemed to improve my condition. My tics were still as bad and strong as ever. As always, I had to be careful of my surroundings and the people that I came in contact with.

There was a movie theater that showed movies once a week. I found out they were holding auditions for a Mexican stage show called an *operetta*. I didn't know what that was, but I auditioned anyway. It was about an Englishman who dreamed of going to Mexico. I had only one or two lines and I sang a song. One of my lines was, "Ah, Mexico! How I have longed to be here." Then I got to sing my song. I had only piano accompaniment.

I had a pretty good voice even as young as I was. There were no tics during my performance. There was another patient who had a voice comparable to mine; his name was Wilford. He was very short and always wore a coat and tie, even when he was walking around the hospital grounds. He was one of the most conceited persons I have ever met. Everyone has a bit of pride about himself, but this guy was ridiculous. I don't know why he was there. I only saw him occasionally in the canteen or walking around the grounds.

My sessions with the doctor were not doing me any good at all. On one of the few visits from my parents, the three of us met with all the doctors involved with my treatment plan. They told my parents that they might find help elsewhere. They suggested Johns Hopkins Hospital in Baltimore, Maryland.

Sometime in 1951 I was released from Eastern State Hospital. I packed my suitcase, but I was not very happy about the move.

We didn't go to Baltimore right away. I spent a few days at home before the trip. My mother had bought a two-bedroom house in Richmond. The address was 906 East 16th Street; it was on the south end of Richmond. I did not go anywhere much when I stayed with my mother. I just played my guitar with my dad. He helped me a lot. I still remembered the chords, A, B, C, D, E, F, and G, but I still could not play a C or an F chord because of my gunshot wound on my left hand. The first two fingers on my left hand would not bend, and that was needed to play these chords.

There was a movie theater about 10 blocks from my mother's house. One evening I walked the 10 blocks to see a movie. I remember I didn't want to see the movie through to the end of the picture. I asked for my money back, but they wouldn't refund it to me.

On the way back to my mother's house, I suddenly developed a new tic. I began to stomp and skip every few steps as I walked along. I was very confused, because this had not occurred when I walked to the movie theater. I was pretty worn out by the time I got home. I didn't mention it to my parents, hoping that it was a one-time event that would go away soon.

After a while I went to bed and fell asleep. I had problems in bed at night. I would bang my right elbow against the mattress; it was a motor tic. It would last for a long time, but I would finally get to sleep. The only peace I seemed to get was when I was sleeping.

I got up early the next morning because of our trip to Baltimore. I had a bowl of cereal for breakfast. I had never unpacked my suitcase, so I was ready—but not very willing—to go. I asked my father if we could postpone our trip. I was really sick of doctors and hospitals.

My father said, "Son, I'm not looking forward to this trip any more than you are, but we have got to do something about your condition." I agreed and headed for the car. Somehow, my parents had bought a car. I don't know how they could afford it, but they did. I am pretty sure that the car belonged to my mother and my dad's name was not on the title.

At that time there were no toll roads or interstates. We just went north on Highway 301. Baltimore is about 50 miles north of Washington, D.C. It would take us over 4 hours to reach our destination. There was a lot of traffic. The speed limit was 50 miles per hour. We stopped a couple of times to eat and use the bathroom. My father did all the driving. Gas was very cheap back then, and it was not unleaded.

Baltimore is a busy city. Several times we had to ask for directions, but we finally found it, and we found a parking space. We went to the administration building. After a lot of questions, I signed in.

Again I hugged and kissed my parents goodbye. An attendant escorted me to my ward. I am not certain what floor it was on, and I did not have a private room. There were five or six other patients on the same ward. My doctor, Dr. Ziegler, finally showed up. (I'm not sure of the spelling. After all, that was 1951 or 1952, almost sixty years ago. I was 17 at that time.)

We discussed my condition. Once more in a long line of meetings like this, I told him about my doctors, my medications, and my hospital stays. He agreed with me that I had been through a lot. I told him that I was sick and tired of it all. I had no control over my life. I did not know what the outside world was like.

He said that he would try his best to relieve me from my suffering. I went back to my ward, put on some pajamas and a bathrobe, lay down on my bed and began to cry. My crying spell lasted a long time. I actually began praying to God. I was not a Christian believer. To me, God was some old man with a long gray beard and was a million miles away somewhere. In fact, I did not know how to pray or what to say to God.

I closed my eyes and said, "I don't know if you can hear me, but I need help. My life is a real mess, and I really need your help, so if you are real, please, please take away whatever this thing is that is controlling my life. Amen." There was dead silence, except for a nurse running back and forth passing out medications.

It was lunchtime, and they brought your food to you. There was no dining room and no standing in line like Eastern State Hospital. Much to my delight, the food was really good. I don't recall what I had, but it was way better than Eastern State. You got to choose from a menu. I am sure my parents were paying through the nose for this hospital. There was a pool table on one of the upper floors. I was told that I could play any time I wanted to.

There were some fine-looking nurses on my ward. I would masturbate at night when everybody was asleep.

I did go to the recreation room to play pool, but an attendant went everywhere with me. There were not too many places to go without an attendant. The only time I was alone was in the bathroom.

After a series of visits with my doctor, I was told that I would be put on insulin shock therapy. I didn't have a clue as to what that was. When my doctor said *shock*, I immediately thought of Eastern State and Tuckers Hospital. I did not want to go through that hell again. I asked my doctor if it was anything like Electric Shock Therapy. He assured me that it was nowhere close to it.

"First of all," he continued, "there will be no electricity used." He explained that I would be given large doses of insulin and I would go into a deep coma for about an hour.

I said, "I thought insulin was only for diabetics."

He said, "It is, but in much smaller doses." He assured me that it was safe.

I said, "OK, Doc, but I am not looking forward to it."

He laughed and said, "You'll be all right. A nurse will be watching you all the time." He also told me that I would receive one treatment every other day.

On the first day of my treatment I had no breakfast. I lay down on my bed, and the nurse put a tourniquet around my left arm and began injecting the insulin. It did not take long for me to become comatose. I was looking at the ceiling—and then there was total darkness. I don't know how long I was out, but when I woke up there was a large needle pumping something into my arm. I asked the nurse what it was. She said that it was glucose, or sugar water. She said it would counteract the insulin and revive me when the bottle was empty. She carefully took the needle out of my arm. She also told me to be aware of an insulin reaction. I asked what the signs were; she said to watch out for things like sweating, double vision, and intense thirst.

A couple of days later I was brushing my teeth when all of a sudden I began to sweat and I experienced double vision. I didn't know what to do. I cried out for help, but I barely got the shout out of my mouth when I passed out. I don't know how long I was unconscious, but when I woke up, there was a needle in my arm again, pumping glucose. Later the nurse informed me that I should always carry some sweets with me like a candy bar, Lifesavers, or even chewing gum. After that, I made sure that I was stocked up with sweet goodies. I continued my insulin shock therapy for a long time with no positive results. I don't remember how many treatments I received.

I recall one really strange event that happened. The attendant took me to a room on the upper level of the hospital, where I met two men. They were dark-skinned like East Indian people, and were dressed in suits and ties, and neither had any type of robe. They asked me to explain my condition to them. They didn't speak English very well, and I had a hard time understanding them. After I finished explaining what was going on with me, they began mumbling, putting their hands on my forehead and praying in a foreign language. They scared me to death! I thought they were nuts. I rushed out of the room and told the attendant to take me back to my ward.

Later I asked my doctor who these men were. He told me they were East Indian priests who believed they could cast out evil spirits. He called it an *exorcism*.

It reminded me of an incident that happened to me when I lived in Hopewell. I was 9 or 10 year old at the time. I went to something called a *camp meeting*. The preacher was a little boy named Little David. He could not have been much older than I was. Anyway, he was yelling and screaming about God and Jesus. It was almost like those two nuts at the hospital, but at least I could understand him. He was telling everybody how bad and sinful they were, that they would go to hell if they did not change their ways, and that the only way they could escape hell was to accept Jesus as their Savior. It was a real "hell-fire-and-damnation" sermon.

The whole thing made me laugh. The only thing I thought about God was that He was a God of wrath, and if you made Him mad, he would send a lightning bolt and blow you away. Oh, I went to church sometimes when I was very young, but only because I was forced to.

After the sermon, people were invited to come up and be prayed for. A lot of people went down the aisle and I thought, "Why not?" I got in line.

It took about 10 or 20 minutes to reach him. He would pray and put his hand on people's forehead and give a slight push. They would fall to the ground and start shaking like they were having a heart attack or something. I thought it was a sideshow. When I reached him, he asked me my name. I told him, "Clarence."

He said, "Do you believe in God?" I didn't want to say one way or the other, but I told him that I believed there was a God of some kind somewhere up in heaven, but that was the extent of my religion.

He noticed that I was very nervous, that I was yelling obscenities, and that I was trying to muffle my outbursts. He asked me what was wrong with me. I told him that I had a very bad nervous condition.

He said, "Do you believe God can heal you?"

I thought for a minute and said, "I guess so."

He put his hand on my forehead and started praying, "Dear God in heaven, heal Clarence of this nervousness, in the Name of Jesus Christ." He was yelling at the top of his voice. I didn't fall down like the other people, and he seemed surprised. We stared at each other for a minute. Finally I walked away. I was more embarrassed than anything else. My tics were still there.

"So much for God," I thought.

On one of the few visits to Johns Hopkins from my parents, they asked me how I was doing, and if I was any better. I told them that I was not any better, and I wanted to come home. The tears began to flow. I had been confined for almost a year, and my tics were as bad as ever.

My father yelled, "Come on! We are going to see the doctor." We went to his office and found him there.

My father was very mad. I thought he was going to hit him. My father yelled, "What is going on with my son?"

The doctor said, "Calm down, Mr. Mizelle, and sit down."

After my father had calmed down a bit, the doctor told my parents what was going on with me. He said, "Mr. and Mrs. Mizelle, we are not really sure what is wrong with Clarence. We have tried various treatments with him with no success at all. We have run out of options."

My mother said, "We really can't afford to keep him here any longer. It's breaking us financially."

My father asked the doctor, "Is there any help out there for my son?"

The doctor said, "There is one more thing we might try. Are you interested?"

My mom and dad eagerly said, "Tell us about it!"

He said, "This will involve an operation."

My father asked, "What kind of an operation?"

The doctor responded, "A brain operation."

My father said, "Isn't that dangerous?"

I was letting them do most of the talking. I just kept quiet and tic-ed. The doctor took out a chart of the brain and began to explain the procedure.

He said, "As you can see, this is the brain. It is the most important organ in our body. The left side controls our right side, and right side controls our left. We will open the top of the skull and carefully cut tiny nerves from the skull to the brain, then close the skull and stitch it closed. The operation will take four or five hours. Your son will be monitored constantly. But there will be some drawbacks."

My father said, "What do you mean by drawbacks?"

The doctor said, "There are two of them. First, there is no guarantee that it will help, and second, it is very expensive."

My father asked, "What kind of money are we talking about?"

The doctor answered, "It will cost about five thousand dollars."

My father said, "You've got to be kidding. We can't afford that kind of money. We are just poor people. Isn't there something else that can be done?"

The doctor replied, "I'm sorry, Mr. Mizelle. There's nothing more I can think of. We have tried insulin shock therapy, different types of medication, and even prayer."

My father and mother were silent for a minute or two. They were both in agreement. They told the doctor, "I'm sorry, Doctor, but we just can't afford that much money. We are just working people."

My father again asked, "What's the name of that operation you were thinking about?"

The doctor said to my parents, "It's called a *lobotomy*. Go on and take your son home. I wish there was more I could do, but the lobotomy is the only option left for him."

I packed my suitcase and we left for home. We did not talk much on the way to Richmond. I finally broke the silence by saying, "Well, what now, Pop?"

He responded, "I don't know. I'm at my wits' end and could use a beer."

We stopped and picked up a six-pack. It was almost dark when we got home. I played my guitar for a little while, watched some TV, ate something, and went to bed. I tic-ed myself to sleep.

The next morning I stayed in bed. I had a late breakfast and just hung around the house playing the guitar and watching TV. My parents had gone to work. I watched TV for a while, but that got boring. My father came home early that day and many days after. I could tell that he had been drinking. He wasn't really drunk, just high enough to "get a buzz on." His breath would have knocked over a mule. He tried to hide it, but it was too obvious. He asked me not to tell my mom, and because I loved him, I agreed. I ate and went to bed.

The next evening I wanted to ask him to show me some more chords on the guitar, but he was in no condition to show me anything.

Mostly I played the guitar and watched TV. Believe it or not, the Mickey Mouse Club was one of my favorite programs. I had a terrible crush on Annette Funicello.

Dick Clark's *American Band Stand* was my favorite program of any on TV. Back then we only had a black and white television set. Little did I know that later down the road, people would someday be watching me on that program! I loved to watch the dancers doing the stroll, the twist, or the bop.

My father woke up after sleeping it off. We had supper and watched TV most of the evening. Western movies and serials were our favorites. Shows like *Gunsmoke, Maverick,* and *Rifleman* kept us up late. I did not suffer a lot from tics when I was playing my guitar or watching TV. Some days I felt half-good, and some days I felt half-bad, but most days were miserable.

My parents and I would try to hide my condition from others. We did not talk about it amongst ourselves, because it would have done no good. Some days my tics were so bad that I didn't leave the house. I don't remember how long I stayed in the house, but it was so bad that my parents decided to put me back in Eastern State Hospital again. They told me that they did not know what else to do.

I was very reluctant to go back to the hospital, and my parents felt the same way. We discussed it a long time, but again, the options had run out around late 1951 or possibly 1952.

We headed for good old Williamsburg. I was readmitted at the age of 17 or 18 years old. I was not sent to what was called the *Snake Pit*. I went back to my old ward on the second floor. I got ground privileges again, and began my old routine.

I began seeing Doctor Orr again. I discovered that my sessions with the doctor were called *psychoanalysis*, a method of therapy that used free association. As usual, it did nothing to stop my tics.

Every Wednesday night there was a dance at the recreation hall. They had a big band from out in town. I would sit in and do my impression of Johnny Ray's version of *Cry*. The audience loved it. I got a very big round of applause. Thank God, there were no tics during my performance.

For the life of me, I did not understand why I had no tics when I played the guitar, or was sleeping, or was watching TV. The words I yelled were not done consciously. I did not choose to say them.

One Wednesday night the lights went out. When they came back on, I was caught making out with one of the female patients. I lost my ground privileges for two weeks. When I got them back, I made sure that didn't happen again.

With ground privileges, you could go anywhere on the hospital grounds. There was an iron fence surrounding the hospital. You could climb the fence and sneak off grounds, but if you were caught you were punished.

I left the grounds many a time. Downtown was only a few blocks away. I would go to a record store and listen to Les Paul records for hours. Sometimes I would go to the movies. Even as often as I left the hospital grounds, I was never caught.

My sessions with Dr. Orr were getting boring. All we did was talk and record the sessions. Sometimes I would get furious and skip sessions. I got bored and disappointed with all the unsuccessful results. I continued until around 1955.

On one of my parents' visits, we discussed my condition with Dr. Orr. My parents were very unsatisfied after hearing that there were no positive results. I had been at the hospital almost six of all my teenage years with no success. My father was very angry, but he had a bad temper anyway. With a few expletives, he told the doctor he was really sick and tired of me being an experiment. He said that he was taking me out of the hospital.

Dr. Orr said, "Mr. Mizelle, that is your privilege.

I shook his hand, and he wished me and my parents the best of luck. I believe it was late 1955, close to Christmas.

All of the years that I was in and out of hospitals and treatment centers, my luck was very bad. It did not take me long to pack my suitcase. As we drove out of the hospital gate, I made a rude gesture to Eastern State Hospital and said, "Goodbye!" to the Snake Pit and the terrible food. I was happy to be free, but I would fight this battle for years to come. Often I thought to myself, "Was I really ever free?"

We got to Richmond in two or three hours. While I was home, I continued to play the guitar. My father showed me more chords. Again, my gunshot wound made it very difficult to form certain chords.

If my memory serves me correctly, this happened some time in late 1955. I had been furloughed from Eastern State Hospital early that year.

I wanted desperately to get into show business, so I "got a wild hair" and decided to go where the action was. Some people told me that New York was where it was. Others chose Miami, Florida, but a musician friend of mine said, "If you want action, the Windy City is the place." It was a thousand miles due north! But he was older and more experienced than I was, so I took him at his word and I was Chicago-bound.

I asked my parents for bus fare, but they flatly refused. I had saved a little bit of money from playing around town. I played the rhythm guitar, but I didn't take my guitar with me. In fact, I sold it to have some extra money.

I decided to hitchhike to Chicago. I wasn't sure what direction it was, so I got a map and there it was—a thousand miles due north. I knew if I got on Route 66 I would be heading in the right direction. It took days, and Tourette didn't help. I was deserted at many a rest stop, and I got caught in a few rainstorms.

I remember one ride. It was an elderly gentleman who picked me up. After a few tics, he asked me what my problem was. I told him that I didn't know, it was just a bad nervous condition—and he understood. He took me about 300 miles and said he had to turn off on another route.

I thanked him and got out of the passenger side, but when I closed the door I accidentally slammed it on my left thumb. It hurt horribly, and I yelled at the top of my voice. But he didn't hear me, and he took off, taking my left thumbnail with him. It was bleeding badly, so I wrapped my handkerchief around my thumb. Some kind traveler gave me a ride to a rest stop where I could wash my thumb in cold water. I finally reached the city limits and made my way to downtown Chicago.

My thumb had swollen a lot, so instead of going to a doctor or an emergency room (which I could not afford) I stopped at the nearest bar and ordered a shot glass of gin, and I stuck my swollen thumb in it. It had stopped bleeding but the pain was almost unbearable.

I looked around and got myself a cheap room, but I had to find a job of some kind. My funds were getting smaller—but what could I do with a busted thumb?

I got a phone book and found the unemployment office, and I got a job as a dishwasher in a local restaurant. But I didn't have to start right away, so I nursed my thumb for a week. I only ate one meal a day.

After the week my thumb was better, but it still hurt terribly. On my first day of work I wore a glove on my left hand and did everything with my right hand. It was tough going, but I made it through the day. I got paid every day, and my meals were free.

Now I needed to audition at some talent shows. I could sing fine, but I could not play the guitar because of my thumb.

I got a chance to enter a talent contest. The first prize was $100 and the second was $50. I sang "That Old Black Magic," by Bill Daniels, a black soul entertainer—and believe it or not, I won second place!

There were no tics onstage, but backstage before I went on, I was very nervous and my tics were very bad. One of my vocal tics was yelling a racial slur, "Nigger!" I had no control over it at all, but I had to defend myself from the other contestants. Thank God, no blows were struck.

After it was over a man came backstage to congratulate me. His name was Bob Armstrong; he was a man around 50, tall and skinny with salt-and-pepper hair. He said he liked my voice. He said that he thought I could go places, and that he could introduce me to the right people.

He asked me where I was staying. I said, "I've just got a cheap room and a dish-washing job."

He asked if he could buy me breakfast. I hadn't eaten so I accepted his offer. After breakfast he drove me to my room. When he saw the condition of my room, he said, "You shouldn't be living in a dump like this. You can do better." He suggested I move in with him. He said it would be easier to meet the right people if we were together.

I thought to myself, "Why not? It's got to be better than this cockroach-infested room." He said he would be there the next morning and help me move into his apartment.

I said, "O.K, first thing in the morning." He said goodnight and left. I thought to myself, "Boy, did I luck out!" I had only been in town a week or so.

I went to sleep that night with a million thoughts running through my head.

But I was in for a big surprise, and I walked right into it head first, being naïve on the subject. Yep, you guessed it— Bob Armstrong would turn out to be homosexual. (Some people called them queers. Back then I had heard the word *queer*, but I had never met one.)

The next morning he knocked on my door early. Back then I was a very handsome boy, only 21 years old, 6 feet 2 inches tall, and with a full head of sandy blond hair.

When we got to his apartment it was gorgeous—three big bedrooms, a large den and a spacious kitchen, all fully carpeted. He showed me which bedroom was mine, and told me to make myself at home. He said he would see me later—he had to go to work.

I found out later that he was well off. He had his own business—he owned an upholstery shop. Before he left he handed me a fifty-dollar bill and said, "Have some fun—go to a movie, or a restaurant and have breakfast!"

I thought a movie was a good idea, so I watched TV until around one o'clock and took a cab to downtown. There were movie theaters everywhere. I like horror movies, but there were none. I finally ended up in front of the Chicago Theater. On the marquee it read, *Blackboard Jungle*, and *In Person—Bill Haley and the Comets*.

The theme from the movie was probably the first rock-and-roll hit of the 1950's, *Rock Around the Clock*. The movie was great, but Bill Haley and his band took the show. I got all their autographs, but over the years they got lost in the shuffle.

My tics were pretty strong during the movie, but when Bill Haley and his band came on, my tics disappeared. I knew I had to get into show business, no matter what. I saw the movie twice, got something to eat, and got a cab back to Bob's apartment. I just sat around and watched TV until Bob got home around five o'clock. He suggested we go out that night and do the town. I had quit my day job and my thumb was a whole lot better, but I still had to grow a new nail. We went to a Chinese restaurant and put on the feedbag. Bob introduced me to the owner. They had a three-piece band, and I did a couple of songs and got a big round of applause.

Bob introduced me to a lot of his friends. I didn't know it then, but most all of them were gay. Bob and I would go out almost every night, and he would foot the bill. He even gave me a job in his upholstery shop. After a few months he informed me that he, too, was gay, as if I hadn't already figured it out. The idea made me very nervous. He never had anything to do with women, and sometimes when we were in his car he would put his hand on my leg. He never really made a pass at me. But if he could get me to meet the right people, what did I care? As long as he kept his distance, his being gay didn't bother me at all. He bought me clothes and shoes, and a new guitar. He treated me like royalty, but never made a pass at me.

I stayed with Bob six or seven months, and he almost became like a father to me. I never did anything to egg him on. I slept with my clothes on, and I would only take showers when he wasn't there. Sometimes at night he would open my bedroom door to say goodnight, but he never came in. I couldn't understand—if he was all that gay, why didn't he try and get personal? But we shouldn't look a gift horse in the mouth.

From the time I met him until the time I left, most all of the people he introduced me to were gay. And I never met anyone important in show business or music. I would confront him, but he would say, "It takes time."

I finally came to the conclusion that he was just stringing me along, showing me off to his gay friends like some kind of prize bull who had just won a blue ribbon. I was just an ornament to him. He had a good-looking but unwilling roommate, and he was proud to show him off. None of his gay friends could top him. That's why he kept me in the finest and most expensive clothes and took me to the best restaurants in town. He thought I was his possession, and he wanted everybody to know it.

Well, I had to get out of this sideshow as quick as possible. I could not lock my bedroom door. On the last night before I left, I awoke to find him in bed with me and trying to kiss me. He held me down while crying, "Don't leave me! I love you!" He was strong, and I had to fight him tooth and nail. I got an arm free, and hit him in the face as hard as I could. I think I broke his nose. There was blood everywhere.

He got up and ran to the bathroom and stayed in there for an hour or more. It was daylight, and I stood on guard in the bedroom for a long time. Then I heard him slam the hallway door and leave. I never saw him again after that. I packed my suitcase and took only what I had come with.

I called home, and my mother answered the phone. I told her I was ready to come home and asked her to wire me bus fare to Richmond. She said she would, and that she and my father missed me. I hung up and waited a couple of hours for the money to get to Western Union. I took a cab to the Greyhound Bus depot and took the first bus heading to Virginia.

So much for my short stint in show business! I was glad to be leaving the Windy City. But it is an experience I will never forget, no matter how flaky it was.

It was a long ride home, and my tics were pretty bad. I had to change buses two or three times. I got a lot of complaints, and had to defend myself all the way home. But I did manage to buy some sleeping pills to relax me. When I got to the bus depot in Richmond I called home, and my father came and picked me up. He asked me about my trip, and I told him that Chicago was not where the action was. Maybe I would hit the Big Apple later on, or maybe I would find it right here at home.

I had a lot of time on my hands, and nothing to do. By this time, my parents knew that I would have to be very careful where I went and who I made friends with, and that I might get into a lot of trouble with my nervous condition. I would get a little money from either my mom or my dad, and try to amuse myself.

One night I went to an early movie at a theater in downtown Richmond on Broad Street, the main drag. Back then movies were cheap, like fifty cents, and popcorn was a dime. I didn't ride a bus to town because of my tics, so my father drove me downtown to the movie. It was a Bud Abbott and Lou Costello movie—"Bud Abbott and Lou Costello Meet Frankenstein." I loved horror movies, and still do. Well, I saw the movie all the way through. My tics were mild, and I wasn't asked to leave. I wanted to see the movie twice, but my tics got real bad and I thought I better not chance it.

It was dark when I left the theater. It was a warm night, so I thought I would walk home. It was a good 3 or 4 miles to my house, and my stomping tics were not bothering me, just the vocal tics.

On my way home I passed a local drugstore, and a woman who was standing in the shadows stopped me and asked me if I would do her a big favor. She was not a pretty woman, and she was with a man that I did not notice. She said, "Hi! My name is Rosie, and I just got off work at the telephone company. Would you cash my pay check at the drugstore?"

I asked her, "Why don't *you* cash it?" She said she had left her I.D. at home.

I didn't know at the time that I would be committing a felony. Being very ignorant about what I was about to do, I agreed to cash it for her. She said she would pay me for it. I never looked at the name on the check. I just noticed the name of the local telephone company—*Chesapeake and Potomac Telephone*. The check was for sixty dollars, as I recall, made out to somebody.

When I tried to cash it I was refused because I had no I.D. either. But the person behind the counter told me that if I would buy something and put my name on the check he would cash it. So I bought a pack of cigarettes and signed my name and address on the check.

At that time my name was still Clarence; I hadn't changed it to Victor yet. So I signed, "Clarence Mizelle, 906 East 16th St., Richmond, VA." (There were no zip codes then.) I don't know why the person trusted me and cashed the check. It would have never happened in today's society.

I gave Rosie the money, less the cigarettes, and because it was dark and pretty late I caught a local bus home. I began tic-ing on the bus, and barking and hollering dirty words. People were looking at me and laughing at me, so I was asked to leave the bus. I was half way home, so I walked the rest of the way home.

No more than a week later I was at home playing the guitar when there was a knock on the door. When I opened it, there was a policeman. He asked me if I was Clarence Mizelle. I said, "Yes, I am."

He then said that he had a warrant for my arrest. I asked him what the charge was, but all he said was, "Will you come quietly, or will I have to use force and handcuff you?"

I said, "No, I'll go." Because I was home alone, I left a note for my parents.

I was taken to a lockup close to where I lived and put in a cell. It was almost like Eastern State Hospital.

I asked him again what the charge was, and found out that the check I had cashed was stolen and I was charged with a felony called *uttering*. I didn't know what that was, but I was suffering the consequences of it!

My father immediately came to my rescue, and wanted to know what was going on. They told him that I was charged with cashing a stolen check, and that it was a felony. My father asked if I could be bailed out. They told him yes, but he would have to wait until I was tried and the judge would set the bail.

My father said, "It's that bad, huh?" He said, "Don't worry, Son. I'll get you out. But why did you do something so stupid?" I had no answer. So he left to try and find money for the bail—more than likely from my mother.

I was in lockup for a while, and then I was taken to City Hall for pictures and fingerprints. I had never been in jail before, so I was really scared.

While I was at City Hall, a detective on the case asked me if I knew the names of the woman I cashed the check for and her accomplice. I told them that I did not have the vaguest idea who they were.

I could not afford a lawyer, so they assigned me a public defender. When I went before the judge, he asked me how I plead. The public defender said, "Guilty." The judge sentenced me to the local prison here, called Deep Water Terminal. I don't know how long my stay was, but it was long enough for me!

My father assured me that he would do everything he could to get me out. I was put in a "paddy wagon" with five or six other prisoners. My tics were pretty bad in the paddy wagon, and the others cursed me and yelled, "Shut up!" I tried with all of my will to muffle my tics, but I had no control at all.

Thank God, I made it safely to the jail, but just by the skin of my teeth. I was escorted to a cell after a shower. I had on prison clothes with a number on the back.

There was another prisoner in the cell with me. I didn't know at the time that he was a homosexual—just my luck! He was well known around town, and was in and out of jail all the time. I don't know his name, but I tried to stay clear of him. But there are not too many places to hide in a jail cell! I even took the top bunk, hoping that would discourage him. He tried a few times to get to me, but with no luck. Again, this was almost like Eastern State, where I had to fight off sex offenders.

He was soon paroled, and I was in the cell alone. I had not heard from my father, so all I could do was wait. I was escorted to the mess hall for breakfast, lunch and supper. The food was no better here than it was at the State Hospital. I was threatened and yelled at a lot, mostly at bedtime. My public defender never once came to see me.

I was incarcerated for just a few days, maybe a week or more. But my father finally came through, and I went home. Boy, was I glad to get out of there!

But I still had to go to the Grand Jury. The judge wanted to know who the woman and man were that gave me the stolen check. He thought I was a part of it. Even though I was out of jail, I was still facing five years for a felony charge. I was determined to find out who the guilty party was.

After asking around town, I found out the name of the guilty party. The woman was Doris Deerheart and her husband was Jimmy Sparkman. They were well known around town, and they both had an alias. The woman was known as Rosie Rotten, and the man was called Filthy McNasty. They both had a record a mile long.

When I went back to court again, I told the judge their names and their aliases. The judge almost fell on the floor laughing, and the detective and the public defender followed suit. After a big laugh, the judge asked me if I could locate these people. He said it would help my case considerably. I told him I would try.

So I began my search. I used to hang around the Greyhound Bus Station, looking for the woman. One night while drinking a soda at the bus station, I noticed a woman at the ticket counter. Much to my amazement, it was the check woman!

I went over and grabbed her by the arm and said, "Hello, Rosie! Where are you going?"

She cursed and said, "Who are you?"

I replied, "Don't you remember me? I am the sucker who went to jail for you."

She struggled to get away, but I held her tightly. She said, "Let me go!" and called me a few dirty names.

I told her not to make a scene, and that it would draw the police. "And you don't want that, do you?"

She stopped struggling and said, "What are you going to do?"

I said, "We are going to spend the night together, just you and me, and you are going to pay for it."

She did not like the idea, but agreed out of fear of the police. So we got a room nearby. It only had a single bed. She asked if I was going to try anything funny, and I said, "If you mean sex, Baby, don't worry. That's the farthest thing from my mind.

We slept with our clothes on, and I tied our hands together with my shoestrings. We had a hard time trying to sleep. My tics kept us awake most of the night, and I sure didn't make any advances toward her.

All I wanted was to get her in front of the judge and detectives. I had a court appearance at 9 a.m. and we were within walking distance of City Hall. We had coffee at the bus station before court, and I asked her why she did what she did. Her answer was, "I needed the money."

We got to the courtroom and my public defender was there, along with the detective. The judge asked me who the woman was, and I told him that she was the guilty party. She didn't have a lawyer.

The judge asked her, "How do you plead?"

Amazingly, she said, "Guilty."

Then he asked if we were in cahoots with each other. I said, "No sir, Your Honor. I have never seen this woman before in my life."

Then he said, "Do you have any proof that you did this out of ignorance? If not, you could go to jail for a long time."

My lawyer took my defense and said, "Your Honor, my client does not have a police record and has never been in trouble before. He is innocent of all charges."

Then the judge asked me, "Mr. Mizelle, do you have anything to say before I pass sentence?"

I looked at my lawyer, and he asked me if I had told him everything. I thought for a minute, and all of a sudden it came to me out of the blue. I am sure now that it was an act of God.

I told my lawyer, "If I was a part of this, then why did I sign the check using my real name and real address? That should prove that I was not associated with the woman at all! I would be jeopardizing my own self. So I did forge the check, but doesn't that prove that I'm innocent?"

My lawyer said, "I'll be! Why didn't I think of that? Mr. Mizelle, I think you have something here."

My lawyer told the judge what I said. He thought for a minute, and slammed his gavel hard down on his desk. He said, "You're right! Case dismissed." Then he said, Mr. Mizelle, you are free to go. You are innocent of all charges. But you, young lady," pointing to Rosie, "I sentence you to ten years in prison." He named a women's prison, but I don't remember the name of it.

Then he said to me, "Mr. Mizelle, be very careful what you sign your name to in the future. You were very lucky."

My lawyer said to me, "You didn't need me in that courtroom. You did fine by yourself."

I still believe it was an act of God. And then I thought of something I had heard somewhere, probably on TV: "Anybody who defends himself has a fool for a lawyer." Thank God, that was not true in my case!

There was a playground a few blocks from my house. I would stroll down there around 7 o'clock in the evening. They played all the top tunes of the day, and the kids would stroll and bop. You could play horseshoes or basketball, but I just sat and watched the dancers, especially the girls.

There were some fine-looking girls there. The lady that played the records was the best looking one of all, but she was way older than everyone else. I tried to muffle my tics so no one would notice me. I was too scared to ask anyone to dance.

The playground closed around 9 o'clock. I was there the next night. In fact, I was there almost every night.

Sometimes I would go to a bar and try to buy a beer. I was 21 years old but I didn't have any identification, so they wouldn't serve me. Sometimes they would have music at the bar. It was mostly a two-piece band with acoustic or electric guitars.

Other times they would have a three-piece band. Once in a while they would let me sit in with them and play my guitar. I got pretty good, but it was not as good as later, when I learned to play the electric bass. I started off on the stand-up bass fiddle.

Around 1957 I was in a barbershop where a lot of musicians and locals would hang around. The owner was Gene Estese, and he would let us get our hair cut for half price.

There were four brothers who hung around there named James, Donald, Norman and Arthur. James was a real character. He was famous for his strong-arm tactics. He was a Golden Gloves boxing champion and everybody was scared of him. He never lost a fight, so you wanted to stay on his good side! But already at 22 or 23 he had false teeth, and I was one of the lucky ones to hold his teeth when he got into a fight. I almost got into a fight with him once when he made fun of my Tourette, but he backed off when some of my musician friends told him I couldn't help it. He was sort of an idol, and we followed him around. But he died a strange death in a pool hall. It seems that he got into a hassle over a pool game and was shot three times with a handgun. He was dead instantly at 24 years of age. Years later his brother Donald opened an after-hours nightclub called *Mr. Don's*, where I played.

At that barbershop I met a guitar player and singer named Boo Walke. Boo was his nickname. He was a better vocalist than guitar player. He was only 14 years old. We became real good friends. He was the leader of his own band called "Boo Walke and the Rockets." It was a three-piece band with a drummer, another guitar player, and Boo on lead.

They were looking for a bass player, so I bought a cheap electric bass. We practiced a lot. Most of the songs were three chords with a minor chord now and then. I played bass and sometimes rhythm guitar. When I was playing bass, I showed the other rhythm guitar player the right notes so it would not be so empty. I was the better musician, but Boo was the better singer.

We began playing local bars around town for tips in a hat and free beer. Boo and the other guys were too young to drink, so I got an identification card and did most of the drinking. I never got drunk or even high. I only drank a few draft beers.

I never mentioned anything about having a nervous condition. They found out soon enough and would laugh or just kid me about it. I would laugh right along with them.

Boo was the leader of the band, and did not give up his spotlight for very long.

We booked a local Moose Lodge for 25 dollars apiece. That was our first paying gig. We added a mandolin player and a bongo player. I did most of the bass playing and rhythm guitar. We sounded pretty good. The place was packed and we earned our money. We booked a few more paying gigs like school dances and local bars. Also we played for free at the playground near where I lived. We stayed together until 1956 or 1957.

After the band broke up, Boo and I started a new band. We named it "The Rock-a-Teens." It was a five-piece group with Boo on lead guitar, Billy Cook on rhythm guitar, Paul Dixon on the bass fiddle, and Bill Smith on drums. We did the same thing as the other band. We played at local bars, YMCA's, community centers, and wherever we could get booked.

As with the first band, I never said anything about my tics, because it was so obvious. The band members said that it didn't bother them. Of course, Boo knew all about my condition. When I was playing music and singing, there were only slight motor tics.

One time we were invited to practice at someone's home in a housing project. There were quite a few fans there, and the woman who was renting there couldn't take her eyes off of me. Her name was Winnie, a sort of big woman, but not a bad looking woman at all. She was married with two kids and had a very jealous husband. At the time, I did not anticipate that later she would become my wife.

She had a knockout sister named Bobbie, that Boo latched onto. She was also married with kids. One night when I was at the playground Boo, Winnie and Bobbie pulled up and invited me to go for a ride. I don't recall where we went, but we parked in a secluded spot. Boo and Bobbie began making out in the front seat. Bobbie was willing, but Winnie was not. I told them about my nervous problem, and they just laughed it off.

I kept trying to seduce Winnie, but she just pushed me away.

Bobbie and Boo were pretty involved, so Winnie and I just sat in the back seat and laughed and joked. It was getting late, so we decided to cool it. I continued seeing Winnie, and Boo kept seeing Bobbie. Their husbands were none the wiser. If they found out about their wives stepping out on them, there would be fireworks. I could never make any headway with Winnie, so I just cooled it.

One day Boo contacted everybody and arranged to cut some demo tapes at a local radio station. A local DJ named Jess DuBoy was the engineer. We cut two or three songs, one of which was entitled *The Rock-a-Teen Boogie*. Boo wrote the song. It was a simple little boogie with only three chords. I had to show the bass player, Paul Dixon, the right notes to play the song. He had borrowed a bass fiddle. We made two or three cuts, and Jess was on another mike in the room behind us singing, "Woo-Hoo, Woo-Hoo-Hoo." This little phrase would be the most important in our lives.

After we finished, Jess gave us the tape. I don't think it was a cassette tape. I think it was a reel-to-reel.

I heard through the grapevine that there was a record label in Roanoke, Virginia, that was listening to demos. I suggested to our recording engineer that we go to Roanoke and try to contact them. The name of the label was *Cavalier.*

We didn't own a car, so we had to hitchhike to Roanoke. In 1959 there were no toll roads or interstate highways, so we decided to travel on Route 60 West. It was really hot weather, and we were having trouble getting rides. I had to try to control my tics. I didn't want to scare anyone. I managed to be somewhat quiet for 5 or 6 hours, long enough to reach Roanoke. It's about 150 miles from Richmond to Roanoke.

When we got into the city we asked directions, and finally found the Cavalier studio. There was only one person at the studio. We told him that we had some demos and asked him if he would like to hear them.

He said, "Boys, we are going out of business, but I can give you the name of another label that might listen to your demos. It's in Salem. That's just a hop, skip and a jump from here."

We thanked him and headed for Salem. It took only a little bit to hitchhike there. The rides were better on the way to Salem. Back then it was just a small town.

We found what we were looking for. The Cavalier man had told us who to see. It was *George McGraw's Music Mart.* It was a record store. We told him about our demos, and he agreed to listen to them. He was a short, fat man with a crew cut. He limped on his right leg when he walked.

He told us to come into the back room. He had a recording studio in the back of his record shop. He listened to the demo, and for the first few songs he paid little interest.

When he got to the *Rock-a-Teen Boogie* with the "Woo-Hoo" phrase, he played the song several times.

He stopped the tape and said, "Boys, I think that you got something here." He asked if it was copy-written.

We replied, "What does that mean?"

He knew right away that we were ignorant on that subject, and did not pursue the matter any further. He told us that he would like to release it on his label. He called it the *Dorah Label*.

He said he would contact us later. We shook his hand and began hitchhiking back to Richmond.

It was beginning to get dark. The rides were terrible again. I had to try to control my tics. Nobody wants to pick you up at night, and I don't blame them. You never know what kind of nut is out there—you can't see them very well.

We got back to Richmond kind of late. My mom was still up, but my father wasn't home.

"Where is Pop?" I asked.

"God only knows," she said. "I haven't seen him since I got home from work, and that was hours ago."

We watched TV for a while and went to bed.

The next night I went to the playground. I was pitching horseshoes when I heard a horn toot. I looked around and there were Boo, Bobbie, and Winnie behind me in the car. Bobbie yelled for me to get into the car. I climbed into the back seat with Winnie. We hunted for a secluded spot to make out.

Boo and Bobbie got right down to necking while I tried to make out with Winnie, but she acted like that door was locked and she was not going to open it. We did occasionally kiss, but that was as far as she would go.

Finally I gave up. It just wasn't worth it to keep trying.

Boo and Bobbie were up front laughing at us.

I said, "Does anybody know what this movie is about?"

"Not hardly!" Bobbie said. "Let's get out of here."

One night a bunch of us were hanging around Gene Estese's barbershop picking and grinding, and the owner of the shop was kidding Boo about his nickname. He got mad.

I said, "What is wrong with you, Boo? I've had *my* disability all my life."

Gene said, "I was just joking with you, Boo." He asked me if I had a nickname.

I said, "No. It's been Clarence all of my life."

Gene jokingly remarked, "What kind of name is Clarence? We'll have to do something about that!"

Everybody was laughing. I didn't like Clarence much either, and I told them so. They tossed a few names in a hat, and I picked one out. The name I picked was *Satch*. I liked that name because in the movies, one of the actors that played with Leo Gorcey and Huntz Hall was called *Satch*.

I was called *Satch* for a long time after that. I didn't care for it much, so I chose *Vic*. That's what I'm called to this day. *Vic* is the nickname, and *Victor* is the regular name.

The band continued to play gigs whenever possible. Boo and I continued to date Bobbie and Winnie. This was all behind their husbands' backs. I am ashamed of it now.

Winnie and her husband got a divorce, and we continued dating. But her ex-husband Gene was persistent. He would follow us around, write nasty notes and make telephone calls. Winnie had to move, but that didn't discourage him, he kept at it. I had more than a few run-ins with him. I recall one incident where I had to physically escort him out of her house. (She was living with her Aunt Tiny in a small apartment in the west end of town.)

We were dating pretty steady then. She would come to all of our band rehearsals, but we still hadn't "gone all the way." Then one night things got out of hand, and I got her pregnant.

She was not happy about her pregnancy, and she wanted to get an abortion. (She was a Catholic, but she didn't practice her religion.) I was strictly against abortion. We argued over that issue over and over again.

She must have gotten pregnant some time in March of 1959. She gave birth on the 21st of November, 1960. The baby was born out of wedlock.

I remember the night her water broke. She was living with her aunt. Bobbie and one of Winnie's brothers were playing poker. I don't know what time it was, but all of a sudden Winnie's aunt came running from the bedroom yelling, "It's time. Winnie's water just broke!"

Everybody got up and ran into the bedroom where Winnie was yelling in pain. She yelled, "Get me to the hospital. I'm hurting!"

Bobbie volunteered to take Winnie to the hospital. We helped Winnie to Bobbie's car. Bobbie broke all the speed records on the way.

We got into a traffic jam. I got out and began directing traffic. Bobbie was blowing the horn and yelling to people in their cars to get out of the way. My tics were at an all-time high. We finally got out of the jam and Bobbie said, "Calm down, Vic. We're going to make it all right."

When we reached the hospital, Winnie almost had the baby on the hospital steps. She fell down, began breathing real fast, and started sweating. Bobbie was trying to comfort her. Her brother came running over and Bobbie said, "Go find a doctor quick!"

He ran inside, and two attendants came running out with a stretcher. They lifted Winnie onto the stretcher. Suddenly one of the attendants yelled, "Oh, my!"

We looked and saw that the baby was starting to come. Winnie was yelling with pain. A doctor came running out and saw what was happening. He said, "Get this woman to the delivery room."

We were told to go to the waiting room. We asked if she would be all right. The nurse said she would be fine.

It seemed like we waited a long time, but soon a doctor came into the waiting room. He said that Winnie was fine. He said she was a little sore, but OK. He said with a smile, "She named him Danny Boy after Conway Twitty's hit record."

The baby measured 21 inches and was very underweight. He had to go to ICU until he had gained some weight. Winnie had to stay in the hospital for a while to recover from her ordeal.

When I got home there was a message from the band. It said that McGraw had called and wanted us to come to Salem and record *Woo-Hoo*. He even sent us some money to get there. We would have to take two cars, because we had a lot of musical equipment to bring with us. (We had also hired a sax player.) Boy, was I excited!

We told Jess about going to Salem. He said that he would like to go, too. He didn't want to go with us; he wanted to fly.

The next day we all met at the Wezel radio station. We left from there and headed for Salem. We got to Salem late that afternoon, and met McGraw at his record shop.

The airport was in Roanoke, so one of the band members drove to the airport to pick up Jess. He brought another DJ with him. We never knew the reason for this. The DJ's name was John Murphy; he was a daytime DJ. They got back to Salem around 5:30 p.m.

We all had something to eat and started recording around 5:30 or 6 p.m. We set up our instruments, and McGraw put a mike on each of us. I was supposed to sing the *Woo-Hoo* part, but my falsetto was not strong enough. We would have had to change the key. Boo didn't want to do that, So Jess volunteered to sing the part.

We went over the song a few times. It was just a simple boogie-type song with a drum break and a rhythm guitar break, but the bass player, Paul, got confused about the notes. I had to show him.

Paul paid only 20 or 30 bucks for his string bass, and it wasn't of the best quality. It would not stay in tune. I had to tune it after almost every take. Paul was not a very good musician.

McGraw finally said, "OK, let's do it."

On his cue we began to play. Jess started off singing, *"Woo-Hoo, Woo-Hoo-Hoo."*

After Jess sang a few lines, the guitar boogie came in. After another couple of measures the whole band started playing.

Our real surprise was that Eddie, the sax player, could play only one note. Our rhythm guitar player, Billy Cook, was OK. He only had to play three chords. Meanwhile Eddie was tooting his one note—which was slightly out of pitch.

McGraw was using a reel-to-reel tape recorder, and he only had so many tracks. We cut and cut, over and over again, but McGraw was never satisfied. I was concerned that Jess would lose his voice. We cut the song almost 100 times before McGraw was satisfied.

We took a short break for coffee, which we purchased from a little restaurant down the street. After we finished our coffee we started again, and worked until McGraw was finally pleased with the take. Boy, were we relieved—especially Jess!

Next we worked on the B-side of the record. It was a slow ballad I had written, called *Untrue*.

I showed everyone the chords. I had to play the string bass, because Paul could not play the necessary parts. We tried it a few times, and McGraw said, "It needs something else."

We decided to let Jess and John sing two-part harmony behind my lead. We cut it a few times, and it was terrible.

McGraw said, "OK, that's it."

I said to McGraw, "Let's do it again."

He said, "Don't worry about it being bad. If the B-side is bad, it will cause the A-side to sell better."

I said, "I bet this is the first time anyone has tried to make a bad-sounding record on purpose!" It sounded to me like a bunch of drunks on a Saturday night.

We packed up our equipment and headed back to Richmond. McGraw said he would get back in touch with us. We dropped Jess and John at the airport and headed home.

It was dark when we pulled into Richmond. Everybody went their separate ways.

The next night I went to the playground. I carried my guitar with me and sang a few songs for the kids. After that I went to a bar up the street and ordered a Coke. They didn't have any music that night.

After I finished my drink I asked the bar owner if he ever had a band.

He said, "Just on Friday and Saturday nights."

I told him that I had a band and wondered if he would book us. He asked me what kind of music we played. I told him we played rock and roll and some country.

He said he wouldn't be able to pay us, but we could play for donations or pass the hat. He said that he got a pretty good crowd on Friday and Saturday nights, and we could make some pretty good money.

He asked me how many pieces we had in the group. I told him there were six of us.

He shook my hand and said, "Be here Friday at 8 o'clock."

I said, "O.K., we won't be late."

I went home and told my mother. My father was still not home. She said that she and one of her girl friends might come and listen to us.

The next day I went to Boo's house. It wasn't very far away. We didn't have a phone.

I told him the news about playing on Friday night.

He said, "Good. We need the practice."

Boo had a telephone, so we called the other guys. Eddie, the sax player, couldn't make it.

Boo said, "Good. That's more money for us."

I told Boo the gig was at 8 o'clock, but we should get there early to set up.

Friday night we got to the bar around six o'clock and began setting up. There was no stage, so we set up on the floor. There was a pretty good crowd already.

We put a donation jar on the bar. We each made about fifteen or twenty bucks for playing that night.

The owner said that we were pretty fair. He said that we should cut a record. He smiled and said, "See you again sometime."

One morning about two weeks later, I was in bed listening to the DJ, Jess, playing music on the radio. All of a sudden Jess said, "Now, here is a local group, the Rock-a-teens, with a song called *Woo-Hoo*."

I almost fell out of bed. I yelled to my mother to come quick, that we were on the radio!

After the song ended, Jess said, "I think that will be a hit for them." He was right. As time went by, *Woo-Hoo* became the most requested song on the radio. The phones rang off the hook.

I got dressed and ran over to Boo's house. He had already heard about it. We hugged each other. We got a call from the other band members, and also from a lot of other people we knew.

In just two weeks, *Woo-Hoo* sold 5 thousand copies. We did a local TV show called Teen Age Party. We began to appear at different places around town. We became so popular and well known that we signed a lot of autographs.

A few weeks later we got a call that McGraw was in town. He wanted us to meet him at a local hotel. He told us that we had a big problem.

He said, "There is a lawsuit against you for using too many notes of somebody else's song." That was an outright lie.

We asked him who it was. He said that it was Arthur Smith, who put out *Guitar Boogie Shuffle*. We asked him what we should do about all this.

He said, "Boys, sell me the rights to *Woo-Hoo*, and that will stop the suit."

We were all quiet for a while. We asked him about how much we would get.

He paused for a minute and said, "The best I can do is two hundred dollars."

We thought that was mighty low. We told him we wanted to talk among ourselves about it.

He said, "Take your time." Then he left the room.

Boo looked at me and said, "I don't trust that character."

We asked the other guys what we should do. They said, "I guess we got to do it."

Paul and I were the oldest. The other guys were real young. They were under twenty at the time. I was twenty-five, and Paul was twenty-two.

I don't remember if the other band members signed or not. I know Boo didn't, but Paul and I did.

McGraw came back and said, "What about it?"

We said, "O.K."

McGraw pulled out two hundred bucks and handed it to me. I split it, and we left the room very disappointed.

Around early August, *Woo-Hoo* was so big that we were called to be on *American Band Stand*. We used the two hundred dollars, plus money we borrowed from our parents, for bus fare and expenses. We also bought uniforms.

Dick Clark wasn't there that day. I lip-synched the record. We went over like gangbusters! We signed autographs for a long time after the show.

Our next gig was in North Carolina, but we were broke. We ended up staying at the local YMCA. In Philly we agreed to put on a show for them for the cost of our rooms.

My parents had bought a phone, so I called home and wanted to talk to Mom. I guessed she would send us some money. Instead I got my father. I told him our problem, and he offered to drive to Philly and take us to our next gig in North Carolina.

He showed up, and we headed for North Carolina. We were booked into a large auditorium with *Santo and Johnny* of *Sleep Walk* fame, the *Crickets, Buddy Holly's Band*, and *David Seville and the Chipmunks*.

Santo and Johnny went on stage, and I played bass for them. We were next. Santo liked to carry pigeons with him. I stepped up on the wooden box to sign autographs, and the box broke! For about an hour there were pigeon feathers and dung all over the auditorium. Santo never forgave me, even though I said I would pay him for the loss of his pigeons. Everyone—except Santo—got a laugh about the mishap.

After the show we headed back to Richmond. We found out that we were booked on Dick Clark's Saturday Night Show in New York City. Again we did not have the money, so we borrowed the money for bus fare from our parents. We took all of our equipment with us. Our drummer, Billy Smith, took only what was necessary.

Paul had to buy an electric bass. Again, I had to teach him how to play the thing!

Jess came along later on. We were at the Little Theater on Forty-Fourth and Broadway. The show was called the Beech Nut Show because it was sponsored by Beech Nut Tobacco Company.

The mother of Billy Cook, our rhythm guitar player, lived in New York City, so we stayed with her. We were booked with Jack Scott, who recorded *What in the World Come Over You*, a group called *The Royal Teens*, Jan and Dean with *Dead Man's Curve*, and a black singer named Jessie Belvin. (Jessie Belvin has passed away.)

The stage was decorated like it was under water. Two girls were dressed like mermaids. Dick Clark would swing down on the stage on a hook, like he was swimming.

We started rehearsal about ten o'clock in the morning and rehearsed all day. Soon after we began rehearsing, I was standing on the stage, and my tics were pretty bad. I was beginning to bark like a dog.

Dick Clark came swinging on the hook. I guess he heard me barking. He said, "Who let a dog in here?"

I was so embarrassed! I tried to muffle the tics during the rest of the rehearsal.

At 8 o'clock we had a dress rehearsal for an hour. The show was from nine to ten o'clock.

We were the last to go on. When we ran out on stage, the house went crazy with applause. We took our positions, and I started the *Woo-Hoo* song. It was all lip-synching. A funny thing happened when Billy started his drum solo. I was supposed to get down on my knees and point to him. Well, I did exactly that. The camera came in for a close up, and rolled over my fingers. I began shaking my finger at Billy. The whole country saw me as we finished.

Girls started jumping onto the stage. We had to be escorted to Jess's car by policemen. The girls followed us all the way to the car, begging for autographs. They even tore our coats off. Finally we got away from them, got into the car, and left.

We stayed at Billy Cook's mother's house another day. We went to Roulette Studio, where the vice president could not stop praising us. His name was Joe Kalskie; he said that we would go on tour soon.

When we got home, everybody in town must have been watching. The phone rang off the hook. After a few days rest, we went on tour.

We were due to meet our tour bus in Chicago, take some pictures, and sign with GAC General Arts, the second largest booking agency in the world. It was October or November. It was pretty cold. We had borrowed from friends and family again. The tour would begin in Chicago, and we would tour most of the East Coast. We left from Eddie's Bar.

Half way to Chicago, the car broke down. A truck driver who had heard of us offered us a ride into the Windy City.

We took a train to get to our producer's business office. He gave us an advance—we were all broke. A photographer took some pictures, and we signed a contract with GAC.

We got on a tour bus and waited for the other performers to get there. There was a good-looking guy named Tommy Facenda; he had a hit with *High School USA*, where he named every high school in the United States. There was a group called *The Passions*, with *Just To Be With You*, and an unknown named Joe London with his first hit, *It Might Have Been*. They all had hits, but *Woo-Hoo* was the biggest of all.

Our road manager was Hal Charm, a real hard-nose. Our bus driver was a baldheaded guy named Jack. We never knew his last name.

We played the Oregon Ball Room, and before we left town we were given money for our lodging. We had to buy our own food out of our weekly pay, which was two hundred dollars for each of us. That was more money than we saw since we began.

The bus was a Grey Hound and was very nice and warm. Everybody shook hands and we were off. I don't remember all the gigs or where they were. We were the backup band for everybody else.

I did most of the bass playing. Paul played only occasionally.

We stayed on tour for a couple of months and backed up some of the big 50's stars. We did the *Allen Freed Show* with Jackie Wilson. He had a hit out called *Higher*. We stayed on tour most of that winter. Everybody on the bus would just laugh at my tics, and that didn't bug me at all.

Our last gig was in Utica, New York, where we were to play for two weeks, but because we could not hold the crowd, we finished after the first week. We were followed by *Johnny and the Hurricanes*. "*Woo-Hoo*" was going off the charts. In November or December we packed up and headed for Richmond. The band stayed together until some time in 1960.

We broke up and everybody went their separate ways. We had a lot of great moments during the time we were together, and those moments remain with us even today.

During this time Winnie and I continued to date, but she had a couple of really bad traits. She really loved dancing, and she was insanely jealous of me. I tried to overlook it, but it was hard to do, and I didn't care for her a lot. We didn't marry for love. It was so the baby would have a name.

We were married at City Hall, but we had an argument at City Hall about her jealousy and put it off for a while. She said she would try to put a hold on her jealousy.

So we became man and wife, and moved into a one-bedroom apartment on Southside. My only income was music, and Winnie didn't work. Anyway, her jealousy became very, very hard to cope with while I was playing on Friday and Saturday and sometimes on Sunday.

Winnie and her girl friend (whom she just called "Sister"—I never knew her real name) would go nightclubbing and dancing. Whenever she came where I was playing she would dance with anybody and everybody, just to make me jealous. It made me more mad than jealous, so she stopped coming.

She would even give our phone number to strangers—again, just to make me jealous. Her sister Bobbie was always against me, and would tell Winnie that she had made a very big mistake in marrying a musician.

Because I had the only income, Winnie took a job as a waitress. We had moved in with my mother and father, who had a house in Oak Grove.

One night there was a knock on the door. It was a policeman. He informed me that Winnie had been raped where she worked. When we got to the police station the police were holding three different men accused of the rape. Winnie was crying and cursing, and I almost hit one of the men. But come to find out, Winnie had teased the three men. She was a teaser, but that was no excuse for rape. They held her at knifepoint in their car after Winnie had gotten off work. The men begged and pleaded with me, but my father (who drove me there) said, "Throw the book at them!" And off to prison they went. There was no trial. It took a while for her to get over it.

We stayed married for a year or so. I had already been on the road with *Woo-Hoo* and was beginning to form *Vic and the Versatiles.* We tried to make our marriage work, but Winnie's jealousy became worse than ever.

I put together another band in 1960. This time I had excellent musicians. We had drums, guitar, two tenor saxophones, and I played bass guitar, which my mother bought for me for my birthday.

One of the sax players, Ross Humphries, also played baritone sax. The guitar player was Zan Agee, and the drummer was Jimmy Trailer. On first tenor sax was Donald Fay. I was the oldest; Ross was the youngest at fourteen years old. He had quit school to join us.

The band was named *Vic and the Versatiles.* We practiced at my house and got real good. I booked a gig at a bar up the street from my house. We didn't make much money, but boy, was I having a ball! I hadn't played with such excellent musicians before.

My mom and her girlfriend came to see us occasionally. One night we were approached by a man named Charles August and his wife, Kookie. He liked what he heard and asked us if we would play for his mother. She owned a movie theater in Dillwyn, Virginia. This was not too far from Richmond. He said that he could promise to have a good crowd.

We talked it over and agreed to do it. We settled on a price for a weekend. We followed him to Dillwyn. He was right about the crowd. The place was packed with teenagers. Again, we went over like gangbusters and signed a lot of autographs.

I think we made a big impression on Mr. August, because later he asked if he could become our manager. We all talked it over. One of the sax players, Donald Fay, said no. His schooling was more important. The drummer, Jimmy, did not want to do it either.

Zan, Ross and I were the only ones left. We would have to go out of town a lot. That's why Donald and Jimmie did not want to be part of it.

I had to find another sax player and drummer. I searched and came up with the drummer who had been in Boo Walker's old band called *The Rockets*. His name was Morris Crumpton. I did not find a sax player right away, so we used only four pieces.

Eventually I found a terrific sax player named Calvin Farmer. He was really good-looking and played a great tenor sax. Mr. August booked us all around town and sometimes away from Richmond.

Winnie and I separated, and finally got a divorce with the help of Mr. August. He was a lawyer, and the divorce was free. I continued to support Danny Boy, but because of the band and my being out of town so much, Danny Boy and I lost touch. He grew up and I wasn't there for him. I have always regretted that, but today we are close. I have tried to make it up to him, and he has forgiven me. He is a drummer, and he works a day job. He was 50 this past November. Winnie passed away in 2008 from a diabetic coma.

In late 1960 or 1961 Mr. August booked us in Ocean View in Norfolk, Virginia. The club was called the *Wing Ding*. We played six nights a week with a jam session on Saturday afternoon. We played until two o'clock in the morning.

The drummer, Morris, was the weakest one in the band. We had to replace Zan, the guitar player. He was real good, but he was always late for the gig, or he would forget his guitar. All he wanted to play was Chet Atkins, and he drank too much. We replaced Zan with a guitarist named George Rosson from Richmond. Finally, we replaced Morris Crumpton on drums with Billy Merits, who was also from Richmond.

Now we were a six-piece band with a great sound. We did James Brown, Otis Redding, and Sam and Dave. Mr. August made sure that we played the top ten hits of the day. We made around one hundred thirty to one hundred fifty dollars per person each week—and we earned every cent of it.

With a lot of practice, we got better and better each month, but the booze and women were plentiful. We stayed at the *Wing Ding* the whole summer and into early fall.

Mr. August bought us uniforms for every night of the week. Ross and Calvin taught Morris how to play the baritone sax and the C-melody sax.

Mr. and Mrs. August would come down on weekends to check things out. One weekend, I remember Mr. August told us that a talent scout from GAC Booking Agency had heard us and would like to sign us up. Mr. and Mrs. August thought it was a good idea.

So some time in the early sixties we signed, and our first gig was in Winnipeg, Canada. It was a couple of thousand miles from Ocean View. We had two Chevy vans and a ton of equipment. It took us three days and nights to reach Canada. We were stopped at the border to have our vans checked for anything illegal. We had to take everything out of the vans. It took the better of two hours to take it out, and another hour to put it all back. We were finally cleared and on our way.

We had a two-week engagement that went over real well. It had begun snowing a few days before we arrived. There was a foot of snow on the ground.

We had a big argument with the owner of the club, who tried to pay us in Canadian money. We would have lost money because of the exchange rate. He finally paid us in USA cash.

The snow was so deep that we flattened the tires to get traction. It took another three days and nights to get back to Richmond.

We played around town, and after a short while we went to Roanoke, Virginia. We played two or three clubs, and finally got a house gig at a club called *Joe's and Johnny's*. We played while strippers danced.

We had rooms upstairs over the club. We were so good that we stayed for a long time. We ended our stay in Roanoke and went on to better gigs. Some time later, still in the early or even the middle sixties, we went on tour, booked by GAC. We were kept pretty busy. We played all over the United States and again in Canada.

Some time in 1967 I got a call from Mr. August, telling me that my mother was ill with cancer of the breast. We were in Kansas City when I got another call that my mother had passed away. It was November 24, 1967. I immediately flew to Richmond for the funeral. Mr. and Mrs. August met me at the airport and took me to the funeral home.

There were a lot of people there. Mom had a lot of friends at the tobacco company. My dad came in crying, and yelling how much he loved her. I thought to myself, "If he loved her so much, why wasn't he a better husband?"

In spite of how I felt, we hugged each other. I have never shed a tear over her death. I don't know why.

In her will, she left me everything. Mr. August was a lawyer, so he took care of everything. It all came to around twenty-five thousand dollars. Her car had to be sold, so it would take a while for me to get the money.

We toured for a long time, and we added a keyboard player. He was from Massachusetts. Any time we were bound there he would come to the gig, and he swore that he would become a permanent member of the *Versatiles,* no matter what! Mr. August was against hiring him, but he was such a good musician. After a lot of hassling Mr. August finally gave in, and we hired Buddy. Later on down the road we added another tenor sax to the band. That made eight pieces—me on bass guitar, Morris on baritone and C-melody sax, Ross Calvin and Gene on tenor sax, Buddy on the keyboard, and Billy Merits on the drums.

We played a lot, and GAC kept us busy, but we were not making any good money. We had to pay our own expenses—hotel rooms, food, and gas for our two vans. Mr. August and his wife kept us in band uniforms, one for each day of the week. Like I said, our booking agent kept us busy. We were what was called a "slot band." That meant we took whatever came our way. If there was a cancellation we would fill it, but for less money. In the late sixties—I don't recall the exact year—we were booked in Lansing, Michigan, at a club called *CD's.* It was the most popular club in Lansing. I think we were making somewhere around $2500 a week, but when you split that, and everyone involved gets their cut—need I say more?

We were the best thing to hit Lansing in a long time. We played five nights a week. We even drew a decent crowd on weeknights, but on the weekends you couldn't buy a seat. Again the booze flowed freely and the women were plentiful. One night we had a small crowd and we were taking a longer than usual break when a young blond-haired man approached us.

All I recall was that his name was David something-or-other. He said that we were very good musically, but there was something missing. He said that he managed and trained show bands, and he believed that with a lot of work we could become one—with his guidance, of course. We told him that we would have to discuss it with our manager, who was a slave driver. He said, "OK, I'll be back for your answer. When will your manager be here?"

We told him he'd be there on the weekend. He encouraged us to take his offer and our money would go up. So on the weekend Mr. and Mrs. August showed up. They very seldom missed a weekend. Again the place was SRO.

We told Mr. and Mrs. August about David and his deal to turn us into a show band. Mr. August asked, "How much would this guy charge for his services?" We told him that money was never discussed. Mr. August said he would like to meet him. He had no more than got the words out of his mouth when who should appear? It was David. We introduced our manager to him. They began talking about David's deal and we went back on stage. David stayed until the last.

The crowd would thin out around 12 or 1 o'clock. We all went out for breakfast, and Mr. August and David discussed our fate. David must have been pretty convincing, because Mr. August agreed to David's deal. We don't know to this day how or if David received any money.

We started training with David two or three times a week. We learned different choreographic steps to do while we were performing. David took the whole band to Detroit to comedy clubs. He asked us to soak up everything we saw and heard. He worked us hard for a long time. He gave us comedy routines to do. We practiced until we knew them by heart, and finally we were ready.

On the weekends, when the place was packed, we put on two forty-five minute shows. I would do an Elvis impersonation. It was set up so that Morris would announce to the audience how Elvis was a poor boy, and one of the band members would be "Elvis before he was famous." Then that band member would go behind a screen, where I would be dressed as Elvis after his success. The band member would go offstage and nobody saw him again. Then I would knock down the cardboard screen and appear as the New Elvis. Ross would take my place on bass. The audience would go wild, and I would sing a couple of Elvis songs. I had on a coal black wig and a jumpsuit. Believe it or not, some females would storm out of the crowd and tear my jumpsuit to shreds!

While I was doing all of this, I had almost complete control over my tics, but they would appear later just as bad as ever. After I finished my Elvis bit I got back on stage and relieved Ross of the bass, and he returned to sax. Then Buddy, the keyboard player would do a comedy routine. He would go offstage and pretend he was feeding the pigeons. Then he would begin singing, "I Don't Want to Set the World on Fire." Billy, our drummer, would come offstage and Morris would take over on drums. Billy would then put a hat with a metal plate in it on Buddy's head, and Buddy would pretend he knew nothing about it. Then every time Buddy would say the word "fire" Billy would pour lighter fluid on Buddy's head and set fire to it. The audience went wild with laughter.

Then Buddy would invite a female from the audience to come and sit in his lap. Buddy did not have a good singing voice, but that made the skit twice as funny. Anyway, Buddy would stop singing and take out his false teeth and try to sing. The girl fell on the floor laughing. I remember one night Buddy was doing his singing to a woman. He took out his teeth—and the girl on his lap also took out *her* teeth! The audience roared for a good fifteen minutes.

There was a knockout waitress that I really went for. I caught her on a break and asked her if she was married, and her name. Much to my surprise, she answered very quickly, "My name is Nancy, and no, I am not married." She was a living doll, real tall, about five foot nine. She had long, fiery red hair and a beautiful figure. She wore a very short dress and her long legs were gorgeous. I asked her for a date and lucked out—she accepted. We got along very well at first. I was wondering how to tell her about my tics.

She was so beautiful, and I didn't want to mess up our relationship so I kept quiet about my tics. Anyway she would eventually find out about my tics—I certainly couldn't hide them. She was living in a motel down the street from the club. We began dating steady, and I moved in with her. She was reluctant to accept any money I would offer her to help with expenses. We were a good team. We fished and went bowling and went out clubbing on my night off.

After a long stay at *CD's* we still couldn't make any decent money. The band was too big and the club wouldn't come up with a raise. We had fired Mr. August, and I still hadn't received any money from my mother's inheritance.

The band dwindled down slowly. Calvin and Ross quit and went back to Richmond. That left Gene Mills on tenor sax, Morris Crumpton on drums, Buddy Krapton on keyboard, and I believe Billy Merits stayed a little while and so did George Rosson on guitar. They would eventually move to Peoria, Illinois, and settle down. They married two girls that they had met when we played there. They both got day jobs at Caterpillar. Gene Mills finally quit and went to live with his wife that he had met on the road. Morris would stay in Lansing and marry a girl he had met on the road. I would finally quit the band and marry Nancy.

At last I got the money from my mother's death, but it was not the 25 thousand dollars I was expecting. We owed Mr. August a lot of money, so I volunteered to pay the band's debt and they would pay me back at a hundred dollars a week. It never happened.

But we had one more gig to play. We booked it ourselves. It was a club we had previously played a long time before. It was a club called *Archie's*, located in Balsam Lake, Michigan. I had fished there earlier when we played *Archie's*, so it was the band's last gig. I think it was only Friday and Saturday nights. After I paid the band's debt and a few other bills like my mother's funeral bill, I had only about 15 thousand left.

We finished playing *Archie's* sometime in the summer of 1969. I know it was 1969 because we were watching the first man on the moon on TV at *Archie's* when the gig was over. We shook hands and hugged each other, and we all went our separate ways. As I said earlier, Morris went back to Lansing to live with his girl friend, Billy and George settled in Peoria. I think Buddy went back to Massachusetts, but I'm not real sure. I think he stayed in Lansing for a while, living with Morris and his girl friend.

Nancy and I decided to head to Florida. I knew of a band that was playing somewhere in Florida. We had played with them in Ocean View—they were called the *Spinners*, a very good band.

I bought Nancy a shiny yellow Caddie—I don't know what year it was. It cost me a little over two thousand bucks. We took our time driving to Florida. Nancy did the driving. I didn't drive because of my tics.

I still had not told Nancy about my condition. I tried to hold them back, but she began to notice my tics and it really disturbed her. I finally told her about it, and that I had no control whatsoever. She told me in no uncertain terms to try and hold them back because the tics were embarrassing. I told her I would try, but there was no guarantee. She was very quiet, and we didn't talk much after that. My tics would drive us apart.

I tried to get some sleep, and she listened to the radio all the way to Florida. It was still daylight when we reached Florida, so we checked into a cheap motel. Nancy was tired after the trip so she took a nap, and I went fishing.

The motel was right on the water. There was a long dock, so I put on some artificial bait and started trolling. I didn't know what kind of fish I was fishing for, but I was hoping to hook something. I made a long cast and began jerking my bait slowly. All of a sudden something hit my bait and almost pulled the rod and reel out of my hand. I didn't know what it was, but it was big and heavy! After about 15 or 20 minutes I landed it. I still did not know what kind of fish it was. It was sort of like a freshwater carp, but it was a whitish color and had a small black spot on its tail. I took it to the motel manager and he identified it for me.

He said, "Son, you've got yourself a nice black drum." I asked him if it was any good.

He smiled and said, "It's terrific good eating!" He weighed it for me, and it weighed about six pounds.

There was a kitchen in our motel room, so I made an attempt to clean it. I was a freshwater fisherman—I wasn't too hip on saltwater fish! Anyway, I cleaned it and scaled it and cut it into filets, and Nancy and I had our first fish dinner. I was still having strong tics, and again Nancy asked me to muffle it. I tried it, but I could not control the tics.

Nancy said, "I'm not going anywhere with you as long as you're making those stupid noises."

I got really mad and said, "Woman, who do you think you are? I've tried my best to hold back my tics, and you're not helping the situation with your carping and moaning.

Now it's *my* money and *my* car, and we're going to try and find out where the *Spinner* band is playing. So get yourself dressed and ready to go."

She stared at me for a long time and started crying. I told her I was sorry, and that she should try to understand my predicament. After all, we were married, and husbands and wives are supposed to support each other. So we got dressed and took off.

I knew the band had a gig somewhere in St. Petersburg. We searched and asked people for the names of popular clubs in the area. After a long search we finally found the band at a club called *The Office*. There was no cover charge; we went in and seated ourselves. They were a very good band, and they played all of the popular songs.

They took a break and I went over and tapped the leader on the shoulder. He turned around and recognized me and shook my hand. "Vic!" he yelled. "What are you doing in Florida?"

"Looking for a band to join," I said. He told me that the union was pretty strict, and that you would have to have a valid union card in order to play.

"Most of the clubs are union," he said, "and they pay union scale."

I told him that I would join the union, but I never did, and I didn't play music either. I sat in and sang a few songs. I didn't play a musical instrument, so I wasn't in much danger. We stayed for a couple of sets and headed back to Treasure Island. It's only a few miles from Treasure Island to St. Petersburg.

We were running low on money. We only had five or six thousand dollars left. Nancy got tired of living in motels, and she wanted to buy a house. We didn't go to a realtor, we just looked around. We had to find jobs fast.

So Nancy got a job as a barmaid in St. Pete. She was good at it—that's what she did in Michigan. She knew how to hustle drinks. She didn't make a lot of money (I think it was fifteen dollars a shift) but the tips were very good because she was so pretty. She always wore a short skirt above her knees to show her beautiful legs. I was a little jealous, but I put up with it because it was her job and she was good at it.

We finally found Nancy's dream house. It was located in Treasure Island, but it was on an island called Terra Verde, just a few miles from downtown Treasure Island and Nancy's bar job. It was a beautiful house right on the bay. It had a marble driveway, and sliding doors. We got in touch with the realtor and he gave us a tour of the inside. There was a full garden in every room. It had three bathrooms and three bedrooms, a large living room, an all-electric kitchen and a beautiful white marble fireplace. There was a large wooden dock in the back, right on the bay, and hidden sprinklers in the front and back yards. Oh, yes—and a two-car garage with an electric door. Nancy fell in love with it and told me that she had to have it! I was reluctant. I said, "We can't afford a house that big."

I asked the realtor what the monthly payments would be. He thought for a minute and said that we could move in for three hundred dollars a month after a small down payment of five thousand dollars. I asked him to give us a few minutes to discuss it. He agreed.

I asked Nancy how much money we had left over. She looked in the checkbook and found a little over seven thousand bucks. I told her that we should find something smaller. She replied angrily, "Oh, no! I want this one. We'll make out somehow."

I didn't feel like arguing, so I said, "OK, let's go for it." We told the realtor that we would take it.

He said, "Oh, yes. There's something I didn't tell you."

I thought to myself, "What now—more money?" I said, "OK, what's the catch?"

"No catch," he replied. "Do you know who lived in this house before you people agreed to buy it?"

I thought, and jokingly said, "Elvis—or better still, Sinatra."

He laughed and said, "No, but he was in music! Guy Lombardo!"

I said, "Do you mean the bandleader famous for *Auld Lang Syne*, the New Year's Eve song?"

"Right," he said. After thinking for a while, we counted out the money and signed a lease. He gave us the key and left.

I began tic-ing real bad, because I was excited.

"Calm down," Nancy told me.

"OK, how are we going to furnish this jewel?" I ask.

"First let's get a bedroom set," she said. We drove into downtown Treasure Island and found a furniture store. Nancy picked out a double bed and dresser that cost around five hundred smackers. They delivered it that same day, and we moved out of the motel and into our new home.

Nancy had to go to work. But first we bought a couple of thick steaks and grilled them. Nancy went to work and I went fishing on my new dock.

The next day I started looking for a job. I looked in the local paper, but I didn't have any experience for the jobs. I don't drive, and that's a big handicap. And Nancy's job had funny hours, so she couldn't drive me around—and she flatly refused to do it. I was beginning to wonder, "What kind of woman did I marry?" She was very selfish—but I had said, *for better or for worse.*

I was out of work for a while. But there was a big restaurant on the island, called The Port-o-Call. It also had a place in the back where people could slip their fishing boats and yachts. I filled out an application and got a job as a waiter. The pay was only minimum wage. Back then, in the seventies, it was only a couple of bucks an hour plus tips. I only worked lunch and dinner. My stomping tic made it difficult to carry food trays. I remember one time I was serving the governor of Florida, and I did a tic and spilled the whole tray of food on him. I almost got fired, but he saved my butt. He told my captain to forget it, and not fire me. "Accidents will happen," he told him. I thanked him and he gave me a nice tip.

I also put together a three-piece band and played a few gigs there. I made pretty good money, and worked and played there most of the summer. Nancy and I were making the house payment, but there was never any money left over. Nancy quit her job and got one at the Port-o Call for more money. It was a tourist spot, and the tips were way better.

I finally got a bass job with a local band. The leader would pick me up and bring me home. So between my day gig and my music gig and Nancy's job we made the rent. But we were barely making it.

And then Nancy began staying out later and later. Our hours were different—she worked at night in the lounge, sometimes until one or two in the morning. I had no reason to suspect any "hanky-panky." I trusted her.

But one night after I finished playing I came home and did a little night fishing. It was really late, and Nancy had not come home yet, so I strolled over to the Port-o-Call to find out why. I didn't suspect anything. When I got to the lounge it was closed tight! "Now where is Nancy?" I thought. I noticed that there was just one car in the parking lot, so I walked over and peeked in the window. What I saw I couldn't believe! Nancy was making out with some dude in the front seat. I could not believe my eyes! The door wasn't locked so I jerked it open and yelled, "What are you doing?" They stopped kissing, and I ordered Nancy to get out of the car.

She said innocently, "We weren't doing anything."

I yelled, "What do you mean, you weren't doing anything? I just caught you!" I was so mad I grabbed the guy by his coat collar and pulled him out of the car. I began tic-ing like crazy.

I was about ready to cold-cock this guy, but Nancy stopped me and said, "Don't hit him. If you're gonna hit anybody, hit me!" I didn't understand why she was taking up for this dude, so I just pushed him away and told him to get away down the road.

Nancy was crying. I said, "Let's go home. You've got some explaining to do."

It was just a short walk to the house. When we got there, I asked her, "What was going on?"

She threw her arms around me and said, "Please forgive me. I promise it won't happen again!" We both began bawling.

I loved her so much! So I said, "OK, I'll forgive you this time, but if it happens again there will be trouble." We made love and went to bed. My tics kept her from going to sleep, so she asked me if I would sleep in one of the other bedrooms. We had bought another single bed, so I complied with her request.

Things went along pretty well for a while. Nancy and I would do things together, like go clubbing at night, or go deep-sea fishing. But it didn't last long. She began refusing me, and I was sleeping more in the spare bedroom than I was with Nancy. I asked her what the problem was, and she would blame it on her period, or she would have a headache. Then she began staying out late, and then not coming home at all. She would stay away for days at a time. I did a lot of fishing, and sometimes I would even pray—but that didn't help any at all. I still had my day job and my music gigs, but I wasn't making the house payments, so Nancy had to make them. All the money that I inherited from my mother was gone. We couldn't even furnish the house.

Then one day I was off, and I decided to walk downtown. I thought maybe I could find Nancy's car—a bright yellow Caddie shouldn't be hard to spot. I was a mile or two from town and it was a hot day. I finally made it downtown. I checked bar after bar, and motel after motel. My tics didn't make it any easier. After searching and searching, lo and behold—I spotted her yellow Caddie parked by a motel, but no Nancy. Now—should I go knocking on doors, or what? No, that was a bad idea! So I left a note on her car and told her to come home, we had to talk. Well, she must have found the note, but she didn't come home for a whole week.

I was lying in bed watching TV one night when I heard the garage door open. She came in, and I confronted her. "Where have you been?"

"That's my business," she said.

I angrily said, "Now wait a minute! Do you think you're in the right by what you're doing?"

She said, "Let's go to bed and talk about this in the morning. I'm tired." So I agreed. I took off my clothes and climbed into bed. She raised up and told me in no uncertain terms that she wouldn't sleep with me. I didn't feel like arguing, so I went to the spare bedroom.

The next morning I got up and she was drinking coffee in the kitchen. I poured myself a cup and said, "Now what?"

She said, "I don't know how to break this to you, but either you leave, or I will. I don't love you any more."

I asked her if she had ever loved me. She said, "I cared about you, but I never really fell in love with you."

I felt like a load of bricks had been dropped on me. I asked her why she let it go on for so long—we had been in Florida for a year!

She said, "I thought we could make a go of it. But to be as honest as I can, this thing that you've got wrong with you—the dirty words and the jerking and jumping—I know you can't help it, but I just can't take it any more. We couldn't even sleep together because of it, and I was embarrassed every time we went somewhere."

I told her that she was well aware of my condition before we got married.

She said, "I know, but it got worse. Maybe you will find somebody down the road, but we are very incompatible."

I was reluctant, but I said I would leave. I didn't have a clue as to where to go. I thought about it, and finally decided to try Nashville. I figured I might hook up with a country band there. I had played a little country, but I was not a country bass player—but I would become one in Nashville.

I quit my job at the hotel and gave the band my notice. Nancy offered to drive me to the bus station. I didn't take my bass or my amp with me. I told Nancy that I would send for it later. At the bus station I tried to kiss her goodbye, but she refused me. Boy, did that hurt!

I had a few hundred bucks on me. I would need to find a job real fast. I knew a man in Nashville who was formerly from Richmond, Virginia. His name was Rusty Adams; he played acoustic guitar.

As always, my tics were dominant on the bus, but I didn't get kicked off. I checked my suitcase and got a sandwich. Now I had to find out where Rusty was—or if he was even in Nashville at all! I was told by a musician friend of mine in Richmond that he was working with Webb

Pierce at a publishing company in a section of town called Music Row.

I asked a bus driver for directions. He told me that it wasn't too far from the bus depot, and that it was on 16th Street. So he gave me directions and I started walking. I found 16th Street with no problem. But where was the publishing company? I found some places that were open—it was the weekend—and I finally got the right information. It was *Whispering Pines Publishing*. I searched until I found it.

It was closed, but the door was unlocked. I went in and heard someone playing the acoustic guitar, and somebody was singing—or trying to sing. I knocked on the door the music was coming from, and somebody hollered, "Who is it? We're closed!"

I hollered back, "I'm Vic Mizelle, and I'm looking for Rusty Adams!"

A man came to the door. He had an acoustic guitar hanging from his neck. "I'm Rusty Adams. What do you want? I said we're closed!"

But another voice yelled out, "So what! Let him come in. I need an audience anyway." I looked and recognized Webb Pierce. He was drunk as a skunk. He was trying to sing to Rusty's guitar accompaniment, but he was not doing a very good job at it.

I introduced myself to Rusty and told him that I was from Richmond, VA. He said, "Oh, yeah, I know who you are. Weren't you in a rock-and-roll band some time in the fifties?" He thought a minute and said, "Oh, hell, yeah! You had out a song called *Hoo Hoo* or something like that!"

I corrected him, saying it was called *Woo-Hoo*, and the band was called the *Rock-a-Teens*, and the year was 1959.

He said, "What in the world are you doing here in Nashville?"

I explained to him that I was looking for a bass job. I asked him if he could help me.

He said, "Off hand, I can't think of anybody looking for a bass player. There must be a thousand or more looking for work, just like you. But you could try Lower Broadway, and maybe you might have some luck. There's a lot of bands down there. It's only one block long, but there are bars galore."

I asked him where this Lower Broadway was located. He said, "It's down by the river."

I said, "What's so special about it?"

He said, "That's where most of the pickers end up."

Webb was almost passed out at his desk. He started to tell me how he discovered Charlie Pride, the black country singer. (That wasn't true.) He also told me that Decca Records was paying him $200,000 a year to record on their label. (Talk about being conceited!)

He asked Rusty to go to the nearest drug store and get a prescription filled for him. He handed Rusty a fifty-dollar bill. Rusty asked me if I wanted to tag along, and he'd show me where Lower Broadway is.

I said, "Let's go!" My tics were not too bad. Like always, they were running hot and cold. As we made our way to the drug store, I let out a few verbal tics. Rusty asked me what was the matter, and I told him that I had a nervous condition.

Rusty drove down to Lower Broadway and said, "This is it." He was right about the bars—every storefront was a bar.

I said, "I guess this is where I'll start."

When we got back to the publishing company, Webb had passed out on his desk. Rusty said, "I've never seen him this bad before. Leave him alone. He won't remember a thing when he wakes up."

I asked Rusty if he knew of a cheap place where I could rent a room.

He suggested Mom Upchurch's rooming house. He said a lot of "pickers" stayed there, and it was cheap. He offered me a ride, and when we got to the house a sweet old lady answered the door. She must have been in her eighties.

I asked her if she had a cheap room for rent.

She said, "You're in luck! I've got only one left."

I asked her how much it was—I thought she would say twenty or thirty dollars a week. To my surprise, she said, "It will be ten dollars a week." Talk about *cheap!*

I said goodbye to Rusty and told him to take care of Webb.

He said, "I have—for more than ten years!"

Mom showed me to an upstairs room with a bed and a dresser. I gave her two months' rent. I had left my suitcase at the bus station, and I didn't have anything. It was getting late, and I wasn't sure how to get there from where I was staying. I told Mom about it, and that I didn't drive. She said she would send one of her boarders to get it. I needed to take a shower, so I didn't go. I gave the locker key to a guitar player who was staying there. I don't recall his name, but I found out that he played on the Grand Ole Opry. He said he wouldn't be long.

Mom asked me what instrument I played. I said, "The electric bass."

She said that I was the only bass player there, and people called in all the time looking for different pickers.

After I had showered I waited for my suitcase. The guitar player got back with my suitcase, and I put on some clean clothes. It was still early, so I asked Mom how far Lower Broadway was.

She said it was a far piece, but I could walk it if I needed the exercise. I thought about it, and decided not to chance it, because of my stomping tic.

Mom said, "Why not ask the guitar player to give you a ride? It's Friday, and he's picking at the Opry, and the Opry is right on Broadway."

I asked him, and he said, "Sure, I'd be glad to!" We hopped into his car, and we were off.

I paid close attention so I would know the way. Mom was right—it would be a nice walk. He dropped me off on Broadway. The Opry was just around the corner. I said I would see him later.

Broadway was really swinging. Every bar had a band, and was packed. The first bar I went into was called the Wagon Wheel, but it was so jammed that I couldn't find a seat. It had a three-piece band—guitar, drums and bass. They were not too bad. So I left and walked down a little farther.

I got to a record shop and they had music. I thought that was strange. It was also packed. Then I looked up at a sign with the name on it—it said, *Ernest Tubbs Record Shop*. There were too many people and they were all standing, so I left and went on down to the end of the block and went into a place called *Merchames Hotel*. It was packed, too, and they had a three-piece band, and they were very good.

On their break I introduced myself to the bass player, who was also the leader and lead singer. I told him that I also played bass. He invited me to sit in, and I sort of hesitated. I didn't play country, and these guys were as "country" as mule manure. He asked my name, and I told him, "Just Vic will do."

His name was Kenny Earl. Man, what a voice! He told everybody my name, and that I would be sitting in for a few songs. He also invited a female vocalist up to sing. I thought, "Man, am I in trouble! I've got to back this girl up on bass, and I have never heard of the song she chose." It was a country song by Dolly Parton, called *"Joline."* I didn't have the vaguest idea how it went. Kenny told me it was in the key of A Minor, but if it had more than one chord I would have to fake the rest, and rely on my musical knowledge. The guitar gave a count, 1, 2, 3, 4, and I watched his chord changes. I knew something about guitar chords, and Kenny was off stage giving me strange hand signals. He would hold up one finger, then sometimes two and three, and even four. But I was following the guitar player's chord changes. I messed up at the beginning, but after a few bars I fell right into it. I even surprised myself! When the song was over the girl singer said, "Good job! You got lost at the beginning, but you fell right in."

I sang a few songs and we took a break. Kenny came up to me and told me that I did a great job once I got started. I thanked him, and asked him what the hand signs meant. He told me it was the number system. I said, "What is that?"

He began to explain it to me. He asked me if I knew my musical scales. I told him that I did. He said, "Then you got half the battle licked!" He said one finger meant the first note in the scale, two meant the second note, three fingers meant the third note. Soon, to make a long story short, while I was in Nashville I learned the number system, and today I use it all the time. It makes any country instrument easy to play.

The band played till 2 o'clock in the morning. They played for tips and a small salary. A couple of the musicians lived at the hotel. They played seven nights a week and a jam on Saturday afternoon.

After the band stopped playing I left and walked to Mom's house. It was about ten or fifteen blocks. It was late, but Mom had given me a key to the door. I was tic-ing a little bit, and I didn't want to wake anybody up. I had no problem falling asleep. I woke up to the smell of bacon frying. I got dressed and went downstairs.

Mom invited me to have breakfast. There was bacon and eggs and pancakes. I didn't know food was included. Mom told me that she helped some of the pickers who were having a hard time. She told me about some of the pickers, and different musicians who had stayed at her house—Eddie Arnold, Chet Atkins, Johnnie Paycheck, and a whole bunch of others.

I thought I would try to call Nancy and get my equipment, but there was no answer. I would try later on. I gave it another try later that night and got lucky. I asked her to send my equipment. I told her that I did not have the money to pay for it, and I asked her if she would pay for it. She grumbled a lot, but finally agreed to send it Railway Express. Then she hit me with a hard one. She said that she had had to pawn my bass and had sold my 20-gauge shotgun to help pay the rent. Boy, was I mad! After I calmed down, I asked her to at least send my amp. She said she would, but it would take some time. I asked her if I could come home, and told her I loved her and missed her very much. She flatly refused and said, "I told you that I did not love you any more. I want a divorce," and hung up.

I spent a lot of time crying and even praying that she would take me back. I kept going down to Broadway, and I was getting good at playing country music. Finally my amp came in, and the guitar player took me to get it. It wasn't doing me much good without a bass.

One night I was walking home from Broadway, and I always crossed the same bridge. While I was on the bridge I was crying, wanting to die. I thought, "I've got nothing to live for, so I'll take the easy way out." I looked over the railing. It was a good 50-foot drop. I stood there crying and praying to a God I didn't know. I got ready to climb up on the railing.

I hesitated a lot, then all of a sudden I heard this voice, just as plain as day. There was nobody there but me, but I heard this voice. It said, ***"My son, this is not the answer. Trust Me. I am the Answer."***

Then there was dead silence, and I backed off. I could not believe what I heard, but it happened, and it saved my life. I made it home and cried myself to sleep.

The next morning around 9 or 10 o'clock there was a phone call. Someone was in dire need of a bass player. Mom called me to the phone, and I put it to my ear to hear someone say, "Hello! Is anybody there?"

I said, "Yeah, I am here."

The party at the other end said, "Who is this? Are you a bass player?"

I said, "Yes, I am."

He said, "Good! You might be the answer to my prayer." He said, "My name is Dick Caldwell, and I need a bass player real bad."

I said, "I'm your man. Where are you calling from?"

He said, "Lake Charles, Louisiana."

I said, "My name is Vic Mizelle, and I'm looking for a band to join."

He said, "Vic, you got a job!"

I went on to tell him that I had an amp but no bass. He said, "Don't worry about that. We'll get you a bass if we have to rent one!"

I told him that I did not drive. He said, "No problem— I'll come to Nashville and get you. Give me your address and I'll see you in a couple of days." And we hung up.

I told Mom about it and she said, "I told you somebody would call!" We hugged each other.

Now all I could do was wait. I went to Broadway a few times, and I thanked Kenny Earl for helping me. I couldn't contain myself. I said, "Thank you, Lord, for the job!" I had a hard time going to sleep. I said to myself, "At last I'll have some money coming in and I can help Nancy, and maybe she will take me back."

In a few days he was at my door. We shook hands. He was a short man, sort of overweight, with a moustache and beard. He drove a Cadillac, so there was plenty of room for my big amp. We put it in the trunk. I hugged Mom Upchurch again, and we were off.

We drove all night, and he noticed my tics and inquired about them. I told the same old story; I told him it was a nervous condition.

He said, "No problem. It doesn't bother your bass, does it?"

I said, "No," and the subject was dropped.

We drove to our first gig. It was a Red Carpet Inn in Louisiana. The other musicians were already there. We took time out to go to a music store and rent a bass. It was not what I was used to playing, but it was a bass. He paid for the rental and said he would take it out of my first week's pay.

We got back to the inn and I met the other musicians and a female singer. She wasn't bad looking, but I wondered if she could carry a tune. I don't remember anyone's name—this was in the early 1970's, almost fifty years ago. We all had rooms, so we got ready and hit the first note at 9 o'clock.

We didn't have time to rehearse, so I started cold. Dick was a tenor sax player—not too good, but not bad, and he sang. The guitar player also sang along with the girl. I sang mostly Elvis and Tom Jones. It was not the greatest band, but we worked steady. From there we played New Mexico, California, New Orleans, and most of the Midwest. The band all knew about my tics, and just laughed them off.

I began sending money to Nancy. I could not get her on the phone, but I kept on trying. I was making $175 a week. I would send her $100 and I would live on the $75. All I had to do was pay for food. Rooms and transportation were furnished.

One time I got lucky and got through on the phone, but it wasn't Nancy on the other end. It was a man's voice. I asked in an angry tone, "Who is this?"

He came back in an angry voice, "Who is this?"

I said, "This is Vic. Where is Nancy?"

The guy on the other end replied, "Who wants to know?"

I said again, really getting mad, "This is Vic. I'm Nancy's husband."

"She's not here, she's working," he said.

I calmed down a little, but I was still mad. I asked, "What are you doing there?"

He calmly replied, "I board here to help with the rent."

I didn't really know what to say, and I sure couldn't do anything about it. But I knew that there was hanky-panky going on. The phone call was getting long, and I was paying for it. So I just said, "I'll call back later," and hung up. I said to myself, "Well, that hussy isn't getting any more money!" So I stopped sending it.

I was having a problem singing. I could not hold a note very long, I had completely lost my falsetto, and I gurgled when I sang. Dick confronted me about my problem and asked me what was wrong.

I told him that I didn't know.

He said, "You'd better go to a doctor."

I told him I would. So I went to several doctors on the road, but with no success. My last gig was in Olympia, Washington. It was for two weeks, but I didn't stay that long. Dick told me that he would have to replace me. He assured me that it was not because of my tics, but it was because of my problem with singing. He said that he needed my strong voice and back-up harmonies, and that was the only reason.

I continued on until my replacement showed up. Dick allowed me to help him with some difficult bass lines. Dick said I could stay on at the inn where we were playing until I decided my next move.

I really didn't know what to do, so I decided to go back to Richmond and maybe get hooked up with a band there. I had saved up some money and a bunch of quarters. I called the bus station to get the fare to Richmond.

The man said, "This is your lucky day! We have a special—the fare is only $98!"

The band helped me pack up my equipment. I would take it on the bus with me. My amp would fit under the bus, and I took my bass on board.

Before I left I got a bright idea, so I called a musician friend of mine in Richmond. His name was Buddy Throckmorton, a guitar student of mine. He was in the band *"The Versatiles"* in the sixties. He was working at a music store in Richmond. So I called and got him on the phone. I told him what had happened with the band.

He said, "Come on to Richmond, and we'll put a band together."

"Good idea," I said, "but it will take me some time to get there."

He said, "Come to the music store when you get in. I'll make some calls here."

I said, "See you!" and hung up.

Dick drove me to the bus station, and I got the cheap bus ticket. My bus was boarding, so I shook hands with Dick, put my equipment on board, and I was off.

I knew it would take a long time to reach Richmond. It would take five days. I thought, "Tics or no tics, I don't have a choice." I took the farthest seat in the back of the bus, away from a lot of passengers. But the bus was packed, so I made the best of a bad situation. Because I was around people, my tics were pretty bad. I tried to muffle them, but that didn't help at all. I finally fell asleep, and that was some relief.

I had to change buses three or four times. It was awful. I remember on one of the buses my tics were so out of control that the passengers began complaining and wanted to remove me from the bus, especially at night when they were trying to sleep.

I remember we were a couple of hundred miles from the Virginia border and my tics were way out of control. People were hollering, "Shut up!" and they were complaining to the bus driver. He came to my seat and asked what my problem was.

I told him that it was a nervous condition and I could not help it. He said, "Wait a minute, I'll be right back."

He came back with a cup of water and he gave me a white pill and said, "Maybe this will help. Don't worry about it."

I took the pill. It must have been a sleeping pill. After a little while I fell asleep and slept all the way to Richmond.

When we got to the bus station my equipment was too big to fit in a locker, so they let me put it in a back room, but not for too long. I went to where Buddy was working.

He told me he had got in touch with Gene Mills, a sax player from *Vic and the Versatiles*. When Buddy got off work we drove to his mother's house, where he was staying. She let me stay there.

We searched for a drummer, and in a few days we located one. His name was Danny Brizendine. He was eighteen, and recently married. We told him that we would be traveling a lot, and his wife did not want any of that. He had not been married very long, and she was really against him traveling. They bickered back and forth, and he finally won the battle. She ran off crying. He said, "Don't worry about it—she'll get over it."

We rehearsed for a few weeks and took off for Michigan. Bud had already quit his job at the music store. We didn't have a lot of money, but gas was cheap.

On the way to Lansing we decided to pull a joke on Danny. We said, trying not to laugh, that there was something we forgot to tell him. He said, "OK, I'll bite. What is it?"

We said that we were all three gay. He said, "Stop! Let me out of this car!"

We were all laughing like crazy, but we finally told him the truth and he got a big laugh out of it.

When we got to Lansing we knew the town pretty well, having played there, so we stopped at a motel down the street from the club we were going to check in. But I saw that it was the same motel that Nancy and I stayed at when I played *CD's*. I started bawling like a baby, so the guys felt sorry for me. So we checked in at another motel right across from the club, the same one the *Versatiles* stayed at. We got two rooms and bunked together.

We set up and began to rehearse. Gene had booked the job for a thousand dollars a week. It was a two-week gig. After rehearsal we got something to eat, and got some sleep.

The next day was Friday. We started playing at 9 p.m. We were supposed to play until 1 o'clock but the crowd was small, so *CD's* let us off early.

Gene had gotten married when he was with the *Versatiles*. He had met her at one of the clubs that we played. Her name was Cecelia, but Gene called her Cese. She was a singer.

Gene suggested that she should join the band. We were all against it. He said that a female vocalist might bring in a crowd. Finally we agreed, against our better judgment.

She arrived after a few days and we began rehearsing. She did a good job and drew in a pretty good crowd. We did the two weeks, and Gene again made a suggestion. He said that she should get a full cut of the money. We really fought him about it, and eventually they both quit the band.

So I took over as bandleader, and named the band the *New Versatiles*. We got hooked up with a booking agency out of Detroit. They booked us mostly in northern Michigan. The clubs where they booked us were dumps. The money got lower, and we could not stay afloat or make a decent living. So after a few months or more, the band went belly up, and everybody went their separate ways.

I went back to Lansing and moved in with Morris Crumpton. He had remained in Lansing after the *Versatiles* broke up. He had also married a girl from Lansing. I did not have a job, so they let me move into their basement and they supported me for a long time. Morris was working as a plumber's helper. He got me a job, too. The pay was not very good, but at least it was something.

One day Morris and the boss plumber and I were having lunch at a restaurant called the *Green Door Lounge*. They had a female two-piece band, but the owner was not satisfied. Morris and I got into a conversation with the owner, and told him that we were musicians. If we put a band together, could we play there?

He said, "Why not! Anything is better than what we got now!"

We needed at least one more musician to form a trio. We decided to get in touch with Buddy Krafton, the *Versatiles'* old keyboard player. We called him and asked him if he would like to join us. He asked what kind of money he would be making. We hadn't set a price with the owner yet, but we told him $150 a week for four nights' work.

He said, "Aw, what the heck! I'm not doing anything here, so I'll take it. See you guys in a few days!"

We told him that he did not have to bring any equipment. The restaurant would furnish him with a piano. He showed up a few days later and the owner let us rehearse.

The owner gave us an advance on our salary, so Buddy and I got a cheap apartment. We started on a Wednesday night. The owner had advertised, so we had a good crowd. We played Wednesday through Saturday, and we kept a packed house. The owner was very pleased with the band. We named it the *Green Door Lounge Band*; our theme song was *Green Door*, by Jim Lowe.

The women and the booze were plentiful. I didn't drink, but Morris and Buddy could put away a lot of booze. But they never got too drunk to perform. They knew about my tics, so that was no problem. When I was playing, there were no tics, but on the break I would tic like everything.

I had my choice of women. I was living in sin, and I was enjoying it. But if I had died I would have gone straight to hell.

One night when we had been at the Green Door about a year, I met a woman whose name was Diane. She was real short and a little overweight, but she was very attractive. She was from a small town in northern Michigan called Alpena, but she lived and worked in Lansing. We began dating steady, and I got her pregnant. She gave birth to a beautiful baby boy in 1972. We named him Chris, but he was way underweight, so he spent some time in ICU. We would visit him, but Diane would not let me hold him because of my tics. She was scared that I might drop him. Boy, did that hurt! But she was just being careful. Diane breast-fed Chris, and I had to wait outside. I really resented that.

My singing at the *Green Door* was not up to par. Only Morris and I sang—Buddy couldn't carry a tune in a bucket, but he was a great keyboard player. Anyway, my throat began to burn, and I would belch a lot, and when I tried to sing a high note I would gurgle! This went on for a while, and I finally saw a doctor. I don't remember all the details. He looked down my throat and found it a little red, but that's all. I told him about the burning sensation and the belching, and he suggested that I have something called an Upper GI. I didn't know what that was, but I agreed.

I was given some real chalky stuff to swallow, called *barium*. Then I stood in front of a machine called a fluoroscope, and the doctor could trace the barium all the way down to my stomach. The Upper GI showed that I had a large hiatal hernia that was causing stomach acids to come up in my throat and burn my esophagus when I ate or belched. My stomach had broken through my diaphragm, and that's what made me gurgle when I sang.

The doctor said that the only remedy was an operation. I waited a while, but the symptoms were too bad. So I checked into Sparrow Hospital and had an operation on my stomach in 1973. They opened up my stomach from my sternum to my belly button, but they cut around my belly button. Then they pulled my stomach down from my diaphragm and stitched it to my sternum. The operation took a couple of hours. Afterwards I was in awful pain. I was out of work for a couple of weeks and the band got a substitute.

Diane and I had moved into a small one-bedroom apartment. She was the breadwinner while I was sick.

When I came back I only played bass; I could not sing a note. That made Morris the only one that sang. He finally quit the band, and we hired another drummer who could sing very well; his name was Richard Snider. He did all the singing until I healed up and began singing again.

Buddy began drinking heavily, and sometimes he could not perform. Anyway, the band broke up, but Richard stayed on and put together another band. Buddy moved in with a girl he had met, named Cathy, who was a good friend of Diane.

Diane was working, but she wasn't making enough money to support all three of us. I was a father now. I had responsibilities. I looked for work but with no success. Besides, I wanted to play, so I decided to call Boo Walke, the guitar player for the *Rock-a-Teens* in 1959. I got his number in Richmond and got him on the phone. I told him my situation.

I said, "I need a job. Do you know anybody who's looking for a bass player?"

He said, "You must have read my mind! I need a bass player real bad!"

I asked him who was playing bass for him. He told me somebody I didn't know.

I said, "Is he good?"

Boo said, "He's OK, but he's no Vic Mizelle!"

So I told Boo that I would hop a plane to Richmond.

He said, "Give me a call when you get here, and I'll send somebody to meet you."

I said, "OK, I'll see you in Richmond."

I told Diane, and asked her if she and Chris would come to Richmond to live. She agreed. My amp was too big to put on the plane, so I told Diane to send it to me Railway Express. I took my bass on the plane.

Diane drove me to the airport and paid for my ticket to Richmond—a straight flight with no layovers. I hugged Diane and kissed Chris goodbye, and told her I would see her in Richmond. I took my bass and boarded the plane. I was in First Class, so I could pick my seat. I tried to sit as far from other passengers as I could, but the plane was full.

My tics were as bad as always, but I tried to muffle them the best I could. I could not wait to get off that plane! The trip took four or five hours, and I made it with no complaints. I tried to get some sleep, but with no luck. We finally landed, and I heard the pilot saying, "Welcome to Richmond, Virginia. The temperature is…."

I grabbed my bass and headed for the waiting room. When I got there a young guy, no more than 14 or 15, asked me, "Are you Vic Mizelle?"

I said, "Yes, but how did you know?"

He smiled and said, "You're the only one with a guitar case!"

I said, "*Bass*, not guitar!"

He introduced himself as Harry Paulett. He said, "I am Boo Walke's drummer."

I asked him the name of the band.

He said, *"Boo Walke and Company."*

He was driving a van. I told him that my amp was being sent Railway Express and it might be there. I was in luck—it had arrived. I had a little money but I was short a few bucks. Harry offered to make it up. We loaded my amp and headed for the club.

It was called *Mr. Don's*. I think I had played there earlier, when it was called by another name. Harry had a key to the club. I put my amp on stage and let out a loud tic—I don't know what it was—and Harry asked if I was all right.

I told him it was a nervous habit, and I could not help it.

He said, "No problem. Boo said something about it, but he didn't go into details."

We both laughed about it, and the matter was forgotten. After setting up, we went to Boo's house. His wife Joyce was there, but Boo was at work. Joyce was no stranger to me.

I had known her back in the 50's when she and Boo got married—they were both very young.

When Boo got home he said, "Glad to see you! What have you been doing?"

I filled him in as best I could.

He asked me if I had found a place to stay.

I said, "No, I haven't had time to look around yet."

He said, "You can bunk on the couch until you find a place."

I thanked him, and we had something to eat. He began to tell me about the club. He said, "It's packed every Friday and Saturday night. It's a late gig from one o'clock to four o'clock, and he pays $50 a man."

I asked him who else was in the band.

He said, "You've already met Harry—he's the youngest. I've got Bert Lousey and Tommy Burgess on sax, me on lead guitar, and you, Vic Mizelle, on bass." He told me that Bert drank a lot, but he was such a good sax player that they overlooked it.

He said that the club was a BYOB club—that stood for Bring Your Own Bottle. He said that Don, the owner of the club (the same Don from the barbershop years before!) didn't serve food and so he did not have a liquor license. He could only serve soft drinks. But he allowed them to bring their own booze and spike their own Cokes or 7-Ups or whatever. It was against the law, but he paid off the law under the table. He had been raided a few times, but he never was when I was there.

We had to play the next night, Friday. We didn't rehearse at all, so I started cold, but I knew most of Boo's material. He was an Elvis nut. He idolized him, and he sang like him.

On Friday night the place was packed. People came from other clubs that were open from 9 to 1 o'clock. The band sounded good, and we did a lot of Elvis Presley songs. Boo sang just like him!

(Mr. Don died of cancer some time in 2000; his brother Arthur died, too, and Norman is the only brother to survive. He is a truck driver. Donald had a son Tim, who was a drummer and played in the *New Rock-A-Teens* band in the early 1990's.)

I stayed with Boo until I could save up some money for an apartment for Diane and Chris when they came to Richmond. I saved up enough to rent a two-bedroom apartment, and I furnished it cheaply. I had a bed and a couch and chair, just enough to get by. I called Diane and gave her the address. When she showed up she had brought a few things with her—the baby's crib, and some dishes and silverware.

I was not making enough money at the club to support us, so Boo got me a job pumping gas at a service station. Between the club and the gas station job I made enough money for rent and food. Diane had not found a job yet. She would take me to work at the gas station, but the band picked me up for the music job. The service station job was a night job, but I didn't work on Friday or Saturday night because of my music job.

Boo wanted to open his own club, so he got a partner and rented a large grocery store and we began to fix it up. I picked the name for it, and everybody liked it. It was called *The Nostalgia Club*.

We all worked hard to get the club ready. When we did finally open Boo couldn't get a liquor license because the club didn't serve food. So he turned it into a private club. You had to be a member, sort of like a Moose Club. Boo had to get a cabaret license, and the members could bring their own bottles.

We began getting a lot of people to join as members. Boo was very well known in the Richmond area. The membership increased and we started having good crowds. Morris Crumpton had moved back to Richmond with his wife Karen, so he joined the band. Bert Lousey had died, and Morris took his place. We did a lot of old songs from the 50's and 60's and, of course, a lot of Elvis! Morris' wife Karen would do a belly dance.

For a while we were the most popular club in town, but because of bad management, and arguments between Boo and his partner, and something about the club not being zoned right, etc., we closed down and Boo lost a lot of money.

I still had my gas-pumping job, and Diane had brought a little money with her, but she still had not found a job. She began to gain weight, and I rudely told her to lose weight or leave. I really did not love her, but I did love my son Chris—that was the only reason I stayed with her. I treated her very badly, and I was never true to her. Back then I was a real selfish rat.

Well, she packed up, and she and Chris went back to Michigan. After she left I started bawling about losing my son. My job at the service station petered out because I had no transportation. I stayed at the apartment until my lease ran out. I had a little money saved. I had a rummage sale at the apartment and sold everything—the money was a big help.

This was in 1975. I played in different bands and worked some day jobs. I was a short order cook for a while, but that didn't last long. I hooked up with a country band called *Sonny Burton and the Statesmen*. We had a guitar picker who was albino; he had solid platinum hair and was legally blind. His name was Whitey Gladdon. Our drummer was Danny Brizendine, and we had a keyboard player named Pete.

We played all around Richmond. We were playing a club called the *Golden Guitar*—we played there a whole lot. One night I met a woman named Joyce. We started dating on a regular basis. She was pretty well off—her husband had died and left her a large insurance policy. She liked the band so much that she financed it. She would buy me all types of clothes, and matching shirts for the band. We were booked out of town a lot, and Joyce always came through with the money.

Somehow we got a two-week booking in Bangor, Maine, but Pete the keyboard player didn't go. He didn't like country music, so he went with another band. We replaced him with a steel guitar picker named Moe Ryan.

The club in Bangor was called *Nashville North*. We played six nights a week with Monday off. While we were there we met a steel guitar picker named Milo Jelloson. He was deaf in his left ear, and played slightly out of tune. He would come to the club a couple times a week and sit in to play Moe's steel guitar.

After the gig was over we headed back to Richmond. Oddly enough, Milo wanted to go with us. He wasn't playing at all in Bangor, and he thought that Richmond would be greener grass.

But luck wasn't with us, and the van broke down—I don't recall where. So Sonny called Joyce, and she sent money to have the van repaired. It was a broken axle. It took a while to find a repair shop. We were stranded for a long time, but we finally got it fixed, and were on our way.

I was living with Joyce, and Milo found a room in Richmond, but it was expensive. I asked Joyce if he could board with us. She agreed, and Milo moved in with us. She wouldn't take any money for rent or food. Milo was a Jehovah's Witness. He had left his family in Bangor.

Moe, the steel guitar player, passed away, and Milo took his place.

I was sinning regularly with Joyce, but for some reason I began feeling guilty about our relationship, and about a lot of other things. So I asked Milo for advice, knowing he was a religious man.

I was playing in bars and clubs. I asked Milo if I should stop playing in clubs and play Gospel instead. He said, "No, you're not sinning by playing music. The sin is having sex with different women."

I tried to clean up my life, but I couldn't do it. I could not "walk the walk." But the guilt was eating me up. I was expecting that lightning bolt any time now, but it never came.

Again I asked Milo for advice. Laughing, he assured me that God did not send lightning bolts down on people. I asked him what I should do.

He said, "You've got to repent."

I said, "How in the world do I do that?"

He said, "You can't do it by yourself, but God will help you. But you've got a part to play."

I said, "What?"

He said, "Pray and don't stop."

I said, "OK," and prayed like crazy. I really wanted to repent, but I couldn't stop. I kept messing up.

Milo began telling me about Jesus Christ and His death and resurrection, but he didn't talk fire-and-brimstone. He said that the Gospel was simple. He told me what the word *gospel* meant—it meant *good news*. I thought, "Maybe there is something to this Jesus business!" He explained how Jesus died on the cross for me—and not just for me, but for the whole world—and if I accepted Him as my Lord and Savior, He would forgive me of all my sins, past, present, and future.

I told him that I did not understand it all. He said, "That's all right. Neither do I." Sometimes we would pray together. Eventually I prayed the Sinner's Prayer. I felt like a load had been lifted off of me. I never felt like that before. I started reading the Bible. I didn't understand it, but I kept on reading it anyway.

I did not understand it, but it made me quit sinning with Joyce, and I slept in another bedroom. Finally I moved out. I even got baptized. In fact, I got baptized twice!

I don't know why my tics didn't bother Joyce, and I felt guilty for accepting her gifts. She was trying to buy my love. I did not love her—it was just lust.

Danny and I quit the *Statesmen* and headed for good old Nashville. Danny got a gig on Lower Broadway. I think this was in early 1977.

I played a few gigs, and hooked up with a country band called the Ken McWilliams Band. Ken played lead guitar and sang. He had a steel guitar picker named Johnny Hogan and a drummer named Randy. It was strictly *country*. Everybody was from Michigan. Our first job was in Key West, Florida, but Ken and I stopped off at Disney World in Florida.

When we got to Key West, Randy and Ken were setting up—this was in July of 1977. Ken met someone at the club who was a saltwater fisherman, and he had a large boat. He invited Ken and me to go deep-sea fishing. So on the morning of July sixth, we went to the gulf and began fishing. (I had to explain my tics, as always.) We moved from spot to spot. We were using cut bait. All of a sudden something hit my line. It was so heavy I thought I was hung up on the bottom, but it was a very big fish. I fought it for about 30 minutes or so. I was tic-ing like mad! I finally got it to the top of the water. It looked like a shark, and the boat owner started to shoot it with a pistol he had. But he stopped short and said, "That's no shark, it's a cobia!" We finally got it aboard and headed for shore. We had it weighed, and it weighed in at 50 pounds. I won a citation for it! I had no use for it, so I had a picture taken and I gave it to the boat owner. That's the biggest fish I have ever caught.

We finished the gig, and the next gig I remembered was in Minnesota. One night while on break I noticed a fine-looking lady at the bar. I thought I would introduce myself. She had a drink in one hand and a cigarette in the other.

I said, "Hi! My name is Victor."

She said her name was Kathi. We talked a while and she asked me about my tics, which I was trying to muffle, as always. I said, "It's a nervous habit."

Somehow we got on the subject of religion. She said that she believed in God and Jesus, and she was a Christian.

I said, "So am I." That's as far as it went.

The next day (I think it was the 16th or the 17th of August) my steamer trunk would not lock, so I was getting it repaired. Somebody in the band had taken me to a repair shop—I don't recall who.

When I got back to the motel Ken was watching TV. He said, "Your hero has just kicked the bucket."

I said, "What do you mean? Who?"

He said, "Elvis just died."

I could not believe it. I began crying for a long time. "Not Elvis!" I said. I watched TV, and Graceland was packed with fans. Most of them were crying, too. I thought to myself, *I hope he is with God.*

We finished the gig in Minnesota. We played some other gigs in the northern states, and Kathi came to a lot of them. I got her telephone number and said I would keep in touch.

The band took a short vacation and everybody went their separate ways. Johnny went to East Tawas, Michigan, and stayed with his wife Lucy's mother. I went to Lansing and stayed with the drummer, Richard Snider. He had an apartment over the Green Door Lounge. He was playing there with his band. He was gone most of the time to be with his girl friend.

I kept in touch with Kathi, and I asked her to marry me over the phone. I said, "You already know about my nervous condition."

Somehow, I don't know how, I found out that I had Tourette. I think sometime in earlier years I tried to get in touch with my psychologist at Eastern State Hospital, Dr. Orr, but he had moved to the Allentown, Pennsylvania, State Hospital. I think it was in 1975 that I got a letter from him telling me that I had Tourette Syndrome. He suggested a drug called Haldol. I know that I took it, but I could not stand the side effects. It's been so many years that my memory fails me.

Anyway, Kathi said that she would have to think about my marriage proposal. To make it short, she said, "Yes," but she would have to sell her house and that would take time. Well, she must have found a quick buyer, because she called me back and said she had sold it.

Ken wasn't playing much, so I had time to wait. I told Kathi where I was in Lansing. I would go down to the Lounge and sit in with Richard's band to pass the time. Eventually Kathi showed up. Kathi stayed with me a few days. We did not sleep together—she did not think it was right, so I went along with it.

Ken began booking the band again, and Kathi and I followed in her car. Most of our gigs were local, just in Michigan.

On one of our time-off weeks, Kathi rented a furnished cabin on a lake somewhere in Michigan. We got a phone to keep in touch with Ken.

Somehow Johnny, the steel guitar player, got our phone number. I think he got it from Ken, but I'm not sure. Anyway he called me from East Tawas and said that he had quit Ken's band. He had booked a house job at a hotel in East Tawas. He had a lead guitar player and had hired Randy, Ken's drummer. He said he wanted me to join the band. I told him I would think about it and call him back.

Kathi and I talked it over and weighed the pros and cons. Kathi said she was tired of traveling and would like to settle down for a while. I agreed, so I called Ken and gave my resignation.

Kathi and I packed up and headed for East Tawas. I know it was wintertime, because it was snowing on the way.

Johnny had reserved a cabin on the lake. He asked why I didn't call him back and tell him I was on my way. I told him we wanted to get there before the weather got bad, and that I just forgot.

We got together and practiced a few times. I didn't know the guitar player—I think his name was Tommy.

East Tawas is a tourist town, but tourist season was a long way off, so the crowd was slim. Anyway, we played until the season started and the crowd picked up.

Kathi had gotten a job as a waitress in the hotel dining room.

I asked Kathi again to marry me, and we got married in East Tawas. Johnny was my best man. I'm not sure of our wedding date. It might have been in 1978—again my memory fails me.

One day I got a call from Ken. He said that he had to turn down a two-week gig—guess where? In Key West, Florida! He wanted to know if we would take it. He gave me the phone number, and I informed Johnny—he was the leader of the band. I told him that he could call collect. He got on the phone and booked the gig. I think we booked it for $2000 a week.

It's a long, long way from Michigan to Key West, Florida! It took us about three days and nights to get there. But gas was not too expensive then.

There were three vehicles—Johnny drove his van with our equipment, and he took his wife Lucy. Randy and the guitar player drove in Randy's car, and Kathi and I went in her car.

When Kathi and I got to Key West, the rest of the band was already there. We had gotten separated on the way down. Motel rooms were not in the deal so we had to find one. It was very hot, and the motel would cut off the air conditioning for a few hours each day to save energy. Kathi and I didn't get romantic too often because of the heat!

On the second week of the gig, Johnny and I got into a big argument over who owned some of the P.A. speakers. We had both put in money to buy them in East Tawas. The argument was so bad we almost came to blows, so I quit. Johnny took one P.A. speaker, and I sold the other one to the owner of the club.

Kathi and I packed up, and where do you think we went? You guessed it—good old Richmond, VA. It was another long drive.

We rented a one-bedroom apartment, and I got a day job as a rod man for a construction company. Kathi missed her kids in Minnesota, and she did not like the hot weather. She wanted me to move to Minnesota with her.

I told her that there was no work in Minnesota. I did not have a trade or a high school education, and my Tourette was a big handicap. We argued about it, and one day I came home from work and she was gone. She did leave me a note, but I already knew why.

I got fired from my job because my motor tics were so bad that my boss thought I might hurt myself on the job. I played in different bands, and worked day jobs whenever I could. I am sure that God was looking out for me, because I never went hungry and I never had to sleep in the street. I didn't have to panhandle, and I always had clothes to wear. It had to be God!

My father still lived in Richmond, and was working as a security guard. He would help me out now and then. But as God would have it, in 1980 he passed away from cancer, the same thing that took my mother in 1967.

I did have a son, Danny Boy. He was also a musician— he was a drummer. But we were not very close then, because I had not been there for him.

In 1982 I was staying with Whitey Gladdon's mother. (He was the albino who played guitar with *Sonny Burton and the Statesmen* band in 1977. I moved in to look after his mother, who was in bad health.)

In 1982 I hooked up with Buddy Throckmorton again. We put together a band called *Capital Square*, and we landed a house job at the *Satellite Club*. (I had played it in the sixties with *Vic and the Versatiles*.) We had a five-piece band, with Buddy on guitar, a drummer named Larry Monday, and a sax player named Johnny—I can't recall his last name. We booked the band for $1100 a week, six nights a week. No other club on that circuit had a house band. We began to draw a good crowd. The club had mixed drinks and food.

Whitey's mother sold her house and bought a trailer, so I moved into a one-bedroom kitchenette right across from the club. I could walk to the gig.

One night I met a woman named Ruth. She was also a believer in God, but we began going together and started living in sin. I explained my nervous condition to her, and she said it didn't bother her.

We began going to a small church together. She would furnish my transportation to and from church and other places. One morning at church the pastor asked for people to come forward to be prayed for. So Ruth went forward.

The pastor put his hand on her head and began to pray, when suddenly she fell on the floor and began crying. I had never seen this happen before! It only lasted a few minutes and she came back to her seat. I asked her why she did that. She said it was the Holy Spirit that made her do it—but that didn't stop us from sinning whenever we felt like it.

We stayed at the Satellite Club for two years, from 1982 to 1984. I kept dating Ruth, and we finally broke up, due to my unfaithfulness.

I met another lady at the club; her name was Evelyn. She was from Hopewell, a small town about 20 miles east of Richmond. We also began dating steady, but that didn't last long—she died from a heart attack in my apartment.

In 1985 somewhere along the line, I married Kathi again, but for the life of me I cannot remember when. I know that it didn't last very long. She could not stand the weather in Virginia, and there was no work in Minnesota, where she wanted to live. For a number of reasons, we just could not get along.

It could have been in 1985, because in 1986 Ruth got me a job where she was employed. It was called Civitan Work Shop for Retarded People. I fit in well because of my disability. I was a Material Handler and sometimes an Assistant Supervisor. All of the clients were handicapped.

I was also playing with a country band called the *Working Man's Band*, named after Merle Haggard's song called *Working Man*. The leader was Chuck Parson. He was a knock-out lead guitar picker, one of the best I have ever heard, and had a fantastic drummer named Donnie Nix. I still play with them today. Chuck, like me, has a lot of road time. He started to play with a band right out of high school, when he was only 18 years old.

I worked at Civitan from 1986 to 1990 and was fired because I was accused of sexually touching one of the retarded clients—that was not true!

In 1990 Chuck and I were asked to back up a local country singer named Teenie Chenault. He was very popular in Richmond. Chuck had joined him at 18 years old and stayed with him for years. He had booked a gig in Maine, and he needed a back-up band. He hired a local drummer, and we went as a trio. It was a two-gig job; it paid $250 a week. I think it was November of 1990. Teenie had a van for all of the equipment. I only took my bass—Teenie had a bass amp.

My tics were really bad on the way. Teenie and Chuck knew all about my condition, but the drummer had no idea what was going on with me. I explained it to him. He just laughed and said, "No problem!"

We got to the club; it was called Stacey's Lounge. Chuck had played there before with Teenie's band, the *Country Rockers*, and Teenie knew the owner. It was the last booking on Teenie's calendar. Rooms were included in the deal.

Chuck and I roomed together. At night after we finished playing, we would go for breakfast about two blocks from our motel. One night when we got back to our motel there was a girl in our room! Chuck aggressively told her to get out, and she flatly refused.

I spoke up, in spite of a lot of tics, and said, "What in the world do you want?"

She wanted Teenie's room number and said she would not leave until she got it.

Well, Chuck and I are both believers, so we definitely would not reveal his room number. She looked to be only in her teens, and she just would not leave. Well, the next thing

I knew, Chuck had stripped down and was as naked as a jaybird, wearing only his western cowboy boots!

I fell on the bed laughing, and the girl immediately left the room. The next morning at breakfast we told Teenie about it, and he almost choked on his food.

We finished the gig and headed for home. I was still picking with Chuck when I got back to Richmond, but I had been fired from Civitan for a false incident.

So I went to work for the AARP employment program. They are like an unemployment service, but they find their clients a temporary job at minimum wage. At that time it was $5.15 per hour. But you also have to look for a permanent job. They help a lot of elderly people find employment, but I was probably the only one with Tourette, They told me it would not be a problem for me. Boy, were they wrong!

My first temporary job was at a marketing corporation. My job was zip-sorting mail, matching and collating material. I don't think the AARP informed the company about my disability. I got a lot of strange looks from other employees.

A lot of black people worked there, and one of my tics was hollering a racial slur ("Nigger!"). I am not in the least bit prejudiced, but I have never had—and still don't have—any control at all over my tics. My manager was a big, fat lady who was the meanest old witch in Richmond, and she warned me to watch my mouth. I told her I could not help what I said, but she would not listen. I only lasted around seven months on that job and was eventually fired.

I told the AARP about it, and they told me I could do something legally, but I didn't pursue it. It really wasn't my fault.

I was still picking with Chuck and the *Working Man's Band*. That was money I could depend on.

My next temporary job from AARP (yes, they kept me on!) was at a well-known hardware store. I passed the employment test. The application called for some arithmetic, and I only had a 5th grade education. I could not do multiplication at all. But the job only called for restocking the warehouse and the sales floor. They needed someone quick, so I got the job. I managed to muffle my tics during the interview. The job paid $6 an hour with health benefits.

I started warehouse stocking. The store had over 50,000 items to stock, and each item has a special code number. I thought, *This should be easy!* But what I didn't know was that you only have a limited amount of time to remember and know where each item went.

There was only one black man in the warehouse. I tried to avoid him as much as possible, although we had a few run-ins.

I met a girl there who worked in the sales department. Her name was Jean. I got to know her pretty well, and we often had lunch together. But it got serious—very serious. We began sleeping together, and she would come to some of my gigs. I fell for her real hard!

My job at the hardware store petered out. It only lasted about six months. It seems that I didn't learn fast enough where to stock each of the 50,000 items, and I was having problems with my "nigger" tic.

So I lost that job, too, but I still had my music. I was living in a small one-bedroom apartment with roaches and mice, but the rent was cheap—only $78 a week. I continued to date Jean, and continued to sin with her.

But I found out she was seeing somebody else. I fell for her, but it was a one-way street. She only went with me for physical reasons.

As a Christian, I should not have been messing around with her in the first place. She accepted my disability, but she didn't accept my love. Maybe I was all wrong in the first place. She told me she cared for me a lot, but she never said she loved me. We would make a date, and she would always break it for some reason. I finally got tired of the whole thing and broke up with her—probably the best thing I have ever done!

My next day job was with a company called the VEC—the Virginia Employment Commission. I was a postal assistant again. My job was to take the mail on a cart to various offices. There were three floors. I also zip-sorted mail. I knew how to do that well. Again, the pay was minimum wage.

My boss was a black lady, my coworkers were black, and most of the offices had black employees. I felt like Moses with the Israelites! Despite my tics, I tried to get steady work there, but they were not putting on any extra help. Anyway, that job lasted almost a year. I had a lot of problems.

I did not get fired from that one. Instead, the AARP found me a permanent job with VCU—Virginia Commonwealth University. VCU is a large college here in Richmond, with about 32,000 students. My job was to keep the parking decks clean, cut grass, shovel snow, and spread salt in the winter. I did not have to drive.

The boss was really hard to get along with. He was a white man, but most of the employees were black. In the morning we would get instruction as to what we were to do, then we would go to an office under a parking deck and split up into groups.

A while before this, I had met a woman at a local Moose Club. You see, after Chuck and the *Working Man's Band* broke up sometime in 1993, I hooked up with a band called Holly Creek, a five-piece group. The leader was a real handsome young man called Jr. His real name was Gilbert, but everybody called him Jr., even though he was not a Junior. The drummer was named Danny, and there was a steel guitar picker who was much older than the rest of the band. His name was Teddy Loyde. He had been Teenie Chenault's steel guitar player with Chuck in Teenie's band, the *Country Rockers*, years ago. Oddly enough, Jr.'s mother was a member of the band also—she played rhythm guitar and sang lead and harmony. I was the senior of the group. Because of the hit song, *Woo-Hoo*, and the *Rock-a-Teens* back in 1959 I was pretty well known in the Richmond area. (Of course, Jr. wasn't even born then!)

As always, I told them I didn't drive, and I explained my Tourette—or I tried to. Jr. said, "As long as you do your job, there's no problem."

Teddy, the steel guitar player, also had a problem. He was blind in his left eye. I think it was a false eye, and he did not like to drive at night, so the band would pick him up, too.

All of that is to explain that the woman I am referring to above became my fifth wife. It happened on a Halloween night in 1993 at a local Moose Club. I was attracted to a very beautiful woman sitting right in front of the bandstand. Because it was Halloween she was in costume—she was dressed like a Spanish dancer, and had the most beautiful hairdo I have ever seen.

I mentioned to Jr. that I would like to meet her. Jr. said, "Go for it, Vic!" I was hesitant because my tics were really bad that night, so I laid it aside.

When we finished at 12 o'clock and were packing up to leave, I noticed that the beautiful fan dancer had gone. I said, "Oh, well. I should have been more persistent."

Jr. got the gig money and was giving each member their share—80 bucks apiece. When he paid me he also handed

me a slip of paper. He said, "Here. I know you want this."
It was the Spanish lady's telephone number. Jr. smiled, and
said, "Good luck!"

That was on a Saturday night. After Jr. dropped me off
at my apartment it was too late to make any phone calls. So
I went to bed, and finally got to sleep in spite of my tics.

Sunday morning around nine o'clock I dialed her
number. It rang a few times, and this silky voice answered.
I said, "Hello, my name is Victor Mizelle."

She said, "That's French, isn't it?"

I said, "I guess so." I told her, "I got your number from
the leader of the band."

She said, "Yes, but I don't give my number to just
anyone."

I asked her, "Why me?"

She said, "You just appeal to me," and laughed.

I asked, "Do you drink coffee?"

She said, "Just about 10 cups a day!"

I asked, "Would you like to go for coffee?"

She agreed, and I named a barbecue restaurant within
walking distance. She knew where it was. Then I forgot to
ask her what her name was, I was so anxious to meet her! I
knew I would recognize her, because she was so beautiful.

When I got to the restaurant she was already there.
I recognized her hairdo. I said, "I guess you're drinking
coffee?"

She said, "Right," so I ordered coffee and we sat at a
table.

I said, "I don't even know your name."

She said, "It's Virginia."

I told her right off that I had Tourette. She said, "I've
heard of it, but I don't know much about it."

I began explaining it to her. She said, "I don't have a problem with that." We chatted for a long time. I told her I was a musician.

She said, "I already know that!"

I asked if I could call her again, and she said, "Any time."

She gave me a lift to my apartment, and I said, "I'll call you."

We kept in touch and began dating. I still had my job at VCU. She began coming to my gigs pretty steady, and we had many phone conversations. Finally I asked her what her last name was.

She told me, "It's Shahinian, Virginia Shahinian."

I asked her about her last name. She said, "It's Armenian." She said her husband was Armenian. His name was Jack, but he had died of cancer.

I said I was sorry.

"That was a long time ago," she said.

We began dating steady. She was like Dolly Parton in that department—she always dressed neatly and wore earrings. Her ears were pierced.

I found out that she had three daughters, Mary, Jackie, and Susie. She also had a son Richard, and a daughter by another marriage.

I told her I had been married four times, but twice to the same woman.

She said, "So what?"

We began to go fishing together, and bowling. Sometimes she would pick me up from work and would have a bucket of minnows and two rods and reels. It was a long time before we got serious—even though I tried a few times, it was "no go" with her.

We finally moved in together at her request. I sold all of my stuff in my apartment. She had a three-bedroom condo in West Richmond. We had been going together almost a year, and we fell madly in love.

She was a cat lover. So am I, and she had a cat named Irvin. We slept in separate bedrooms, and only occasionally fell into temptation. For some reason I began to feel guilty and I would refuse her! I'm so glad God was patient with me.

Virginia went to church with her late husband at an Armenian church. I don't know what their beliefs were, and she never mentioned it. She would take me back and forth to work, and I helped with the rent. She was a great cook and made a lot of Armenian dishes.

We wanted to get married, but I was hesitant. We were living in sin, but that did not bother her. She introduced me to her children, and they were beautiful. Susie was the "baby."

I finally asked her to marry me. She accepted, and I made arrangements to have a church wedding. We were married at the Medical College Hospital Chapel; it was owned by VCU, the college where I worked.

We were married on November 24th, 1994. Her children were there—only the three daughters and their boyfriends. It was the first time I wore a coat and tie! Virginia had on a bright red dress and high heels and her earrings.

We took our vows, and a lot of pictures. Afterwards we went for Chinese food—my favorite.

Virginia sold her condo, and we rented a two-bedroom house. Virginia already had plenty of furniture, so we were set. Our landlord lived right across the street from us, so I could walk over and pay the rent.

Jr. no longer had to pick me up. Virginia (VA was her nickname) took me to my gig, and to and from my job. I stayed with *Holly Creek* for a long time, and we finally disbanded. Jr.'s mother didn't want to be in the band any longer, and Teddy the steel guitar player quit. Jr. refused to pick him up. He had a day job driving for an auto parts store. He could drive in the daytime.

Teddy was on the road with Teenie Chenault for years, but he never paid any income taxes and he was in debt to his credit card company to the tune of $30,000. It took him a long time to pay it off.

While I was working at VCU I had a lot of problems holding back my tics, especially the racial tic ("nigger"). One day my boss called me into his office. This was the longest day job I ever had—over three years. Anyway, he told me that he had had a complaint about my racial slur.

I said, "You knew I had a disability when you hired me. So what's the problem?"

He just said, "We can't have that here. Your job is terminated."

I called Virginia and told her. She quickly came to the job site and said, "What is going on here?"

My boss told her that I was fired. She took up for me, and an argument broke out between her and my manager. He told us to get off the property or he would have us forced off.

I told Virginia, "Let's go, Baby. It's not worth it."

She was fighting mad. When we got home, Virginia said, "Don't worry, Honey. You'll find another job."

I was out of work for a while and didn't have a band to play with, so VA was paying the bills. I got unemployment for a while, and I was a few years short of Social Security. (I was only sixty years old, so I took it early, at sixty-two. Thank God, I had worked day jobs and paid into Social Security, or I would be up the creek (not *Holly Creek!*) without a paddle.)

I went back to the AARP and they got me a job at the Goodwill Industries. This was in 1994 or 1995. VA took me to Goodwill and I was filled in on what my job was. I would sort clothes, and put price tags on new clothes that were going to different outlets. I also unloaded large steel cages of old clothes and put them on a conveyer belt to be bundled and sent to Third World countries. I did a lot of different jobs, and some of it was mighty hard.

The AARP had told the people at Goodwill that I had a disability, but Tourette was never mentioned. My supervisor was black, and her supervisor was black. In fact, the whole place was 80% black. My supervisor was a real witch; I mean she was on my case every day. I was only allowed to work 4 hours a day at minimum wage. I got paid every two weeks; after taxes it was around $160.

But I got lucky. Jr. called me. He had joined a country band called *High Cotton*, and they needed a bass player. I told VA about it and she said, "Take it! We can use the money."

The leader of the band was Nelson Elam, a schoolteacher and a football coach. In fact, he was Chuck Parsons' football coach in high school. He was a running back in college and was picked up by the Dallas Cowboys, but he turned the job down because he had claustrophobia and would not fly on an airplane. He still regrets it today.

Anyway, I joined the band. Jr. played lead guitar and sang, and we had a real good drummer named Maurice Semster. Nelson (everybody called him *Coach*) sang a good lead and harmony, and guess who was on steel guitar? Nobody else but Teddy Loyde, and yours truly on bass.

We played a lot. Coach did all the booking. Most of the time VA would take me to the gig, and sometimes Jr. (his last name is Blackburn) or Coach would.

My job at Goodwill was no picnic, either. My black supervisor was continually reprimanding me for my tics or racial slurs. It was not really a racial slur, because I am not the least big prejudiced. I even went to her supervisor and tried to explain. But I was only told to try to control my tic, or I could get into serious trouble. Then the matter was dropped. I was not fired, because that would be prejudice on their parts.

There were a lot of times that I just wanted to quit, but that's no answer, I thought. Besides, I needed the money. I was still too young for Social Security. I had two years to go before I was 62, so I was really up against the wall. I wanted to quit, but could I find other employment?

I asked the AARP to put me elsewhere, but they said that there were no other jobs available. So I was kind of stuck there. There were a lot of shaky incidents, even dangerous ones. Sometimes I thought I would have to fight my way out, but luckily I never had to.

Virginia stopped taking me to my day job because it was a long drive. We lived in the West End, and Goodwill was in the South Side. I did not understand that at all. She just took me to a bus stop. I had to take two different buses to work. I was not looking forward to that at all.

I recall one incident that took place while I was waiting for my bus one morning. There were quite a lot of people at the bus stop that morning, including some black people. There was also a black preacher, shouting out about Jesus and how we should accept Him as Lord and Savior. I was enjoying it, and I said, "Praise the Lord!" But right after that I tic-ed and hollered "Nigger!"

Then a white guy standing there yelled at me and said angrily, "Why do you say, 'Praise the Lord' and then call somebody a nigger?"

I told him that I could not help it, and tried to explain to him that I had no control, and I did not mean anything by it. I really got up in his face. (I was wrong.) And he cursed and said, "You knew what you were saying!"

We got into a heated argument and he pushed me hard out into the street. I fell backward in the street. I was so mad that I was ready to fight. I started to kick him where it would do the most damage. But much to my amazement the preacher stopped me and said, "Don't do it, Brother!" and we hugged each other.

I apologized to the guy and said, "God bless you."

He said, "I don't believe in God," and caught his bus.

A couple of black people who worked at Goodwill were waiting for the bus and they said, "You did the right thing by apologizing. God will bless you for it."

I thanked them and caught my bus.

I stayed at Goodwill almost ten years, from 1994 to 2004. I took Social Security at age 62 and quit Goodwill. It just got so difficult. But I still played music.

Virginia and I were having marriage problems. One of my tics really bugged her. It was a motor tic—it made me sniff real hard, and sometimes some mucus would fly out. For some reason I would turn toward VA and sniff real hard, and the mucus would get on her. She would get furious, and we would get into a big argument. I told her I couldn't help it, and she said, "Maybe not, but you don't have to aim it at *me!*" She was right, and I was wrong. Tourette makes me do crazy things. It seems like I always do the very worst thing I can do, like the racial slur, or snorting like a pig.

The skipping and stomping tics are really a hassle when I am walking. I can't run at all. I have fallen many a time when running to catch a bus, and hurt my knee. I am in mortal danger on a city bus, and that is my only way of getting anywhere. Most of the time I am the only white person on the bus, and I really have to muffle my tics. I have been escorted off the bus by the police. Richmond is 50% or 60% black, so I can get into serious trouble. So I stay mostly to myself.

Virginia and I were having our problems. I have a terrible temper, and so did Virginia. I never hit her, though I often felt like it. I am not the Christian that I would like to be, and any time I would mention God to Virginia she would yell, "Don't preach to me!" She was very stubborn; things always had to go her way.

She had told me at the beginning of our relationship that she accepted my Tourette condition, but I am sure the tics had a lot to do with the end of our marriage. She told me that she wanted a divorce, and I had to move out. But I had nowhere to go.

We stopped sleeping together. We became complete strangers and rarely spoke to each other. She still cooked our meals, but she stayed in her bedroom most of the time, and I just watched TV most of the day.

She found me an apartment from the newspaper, and I moved out. I don't know why, but she put up my security deposit for the apartment. It was $400. And she took me over to move in. It was a dump on the second floor, with no elevator. It had a living room, a small kitchen and a bathroom—and yes, cockroaches, too. It had a gas stove, and it took a long time to get it turned on. It cost me to turn it on. I also had to get a phone, and that took time, too. The rent was $425 a month for that dump. I was lucky I was getting regular Social Security checks.

Our divorce was final in 1999, and Virginia paid for it. This was my longest marriage—five years. There were good times and bad times.

We still kept in touch by phone, and occasionally went out to eat. We went to her daughter's house on Christmas for Christmas dinner. I still think of her children as my stepdaughters.

Believe it or not, after our divorce Virginia and I became the best of friends, and we never went to bed without calling and saying goodnight. We were still in love, in spite of the divorce, but we just couldn't live together as man and wife. We were never unfaithful to each other, and we never remarried.

I told the Coach about my change of address when I moved into the dump, and he began to pick me up and take me to the gigs and bring me home. I had to help with the gas. He didn't like to come into town—he lived in the country, a long way from where I lived, but he continued.

I had to find another place to live. That dump that I lived in got so expensive that I couldn't afford it any longer, so I decided to find a cheaper apartment. But I had to wait until my lease was up. The rent went up $25 every year, and by the time I left it was $475 a month. I did not get my security deposit back—they sent me a letter and informed me that I owed *them* money, more than my deposit! They named off things that were wrong with the apartment. Naturally I refused to pay, and I called them and told them so, and I told them to take me to court. But I never heard any more about it.

Two blocks from the dump I lived in is a 12-story building and apartment complex. It is a subsidized housing project, and most of the residents are seniors living on Social Security, like myself. So I filled out an application. They have a four- to six-month waiting list, and your rent is based on your income. It's sponsored by HUD, and they pay part of your rent.

Well, I had a little while until my lease was up, but an apartment became available before the waiting period was up. So I got an apartment on the ninth floor. The reason was that the person moved out without paying the rent. My yearly income was very low, so my rent was real low. I had quit my day job, and my only income was Social Security and my music money. My Social Security was around $6000 a year, but I didn't include my music money. I was wrong in doing that, but I needed to live as cheaply as I could, from paycheck to paycheck.

Virginia had given me some furniture and a TV. I bought a couch and a chair from Goodwill. In June of 2006 I moved in. I had one bedroom, a large living room, a big kitchen, and a bath. The floor was carpeted. Oh, yes, there were still some cockroaches! It was air-conditioned, and the stove was electric. This was a whole lot better than the dump I lived in before!

When I moved in my rent was $230 a month, and cable TV was $10 a month. That was $240 a month! There was a large grocery store right across the street, and I was one block from the bus stop.

Right after I moved in, the High Cotton band split up, so I lost that money anyway, but Coach came through. He heard about a band that needed a bass player.

I knew the leader well, so I called him up. His name is Alan Lamb. He played lead guitar and sang. He had already gotten in touch with a keyboard player named David Aldrich, whom I did not know. Our drummer at the time was Wayne Boswell. I didn't have to audition, but the group wasn't country—far from it! It was the Eagles, the Doobie Brothers, a lot of 60's and 70's and some 50's Do-Wop, which I was familiar with. We practiced at the keyboard player's house.

Alan knew that I had a disability and he told the other band members. They had no problem with it. We rehearsed for a month before booking gigs. Alan did the booking. The band was called E-Z Knights. Alan picked the name. The band members were seasoned musicians with 30 or more years of experience. I was the oldest member, and I had 50 years experience, with 25 on the road. The drummer was the "baby." He was in his early 30's. We had a fantastic sound, and began playing around town a lot, mostly at Moose Clubs.

I lost Virginia to lung cancer on August 15, 2007. She smoked a carton of cigarettes a week. I tried to get her to quit, but she would not do it. She was 69 years old. We loved each other more apart than we did when we were man and wife. Oh, God! Do I miss the phone calls and the togetherness we had in her last days on earth! I will love her and the memory of her until I go to be with the Lord. But the Lord gives, and the Lord takes away. I miss her very much, and I believe I will see her again in heaven. I have grown very close to God and Jesus. I have no doubts that I am saved.

I did the eulogy at the funeral. She had a closed casket. I have cried so many tears over the years. I still love her dearly. To this day I don't know if she knew the Lord or not, but I pray that she did, and that I will see her again someday after I'm gone.

In my will I stated that I wanted to be cremated and my ashes spread over her grave. I have never dated another woman since she died. I miss her more than I can say. I still wear my wedding band today.

Well, that's about it. I've tried to put 70 years into five or six months. It is 2010 as I write this. I'm 75 years old and I am as close to the Lord as I have ever been before. I don't attend any church because of my tics, but I go to Bible Study almost every Friday. I have to leave early sometimes, when the keyboard player comes to pick me up for a gig.

My Bible Study teacher is Madeline, and she is my "ghost writer." She took the time to type my manuscript. She has been an inspiration to me, and it's her teaching about the Lord and His love that helped me to trust God with all of my heart.

I went to a psychologist for almost ten years here at the Medical College Hospital, and it was just like Eastern State Hospital years ago—no help at all. I have been on so many medications in my life that I can't count them. My tics have receded over the years, but it is still hell every day. I guess I will always have Tourette. ***That's what makes me tic!***

Well, that's my story. I still suffer with Tourette and I will probably die with it. But I have survived 75 years with it, and maybe my story will help someone else with Tourette.

There is a P.S. to this tale of woe and hell on earth. I am 75 years old now, and in good physical and spiritual health. Like I said, I suffer a lot with this malady, and I have decided to leave my body to science, in hopes that someday they will find a cure for this dreaded and incurable disease. There is no information on how many people suffer from Tourette, but my heart goes out to all of them.

I have acquired a new tic that is as bad or worse than the profanity of the past. It's a racial slur, "Nigger." I don't know when it began, but it has caused me a lot of problems. I have been threatened, laughed at, escorted off of buses, kicked out of movies, fired from day jobs, and a number of other incidents. But somehow, with the help of the Lord, I have survived.

I am certainly not prejudiced in any way against black people, but every time I try to explain my disease to them they just don't want to hear it. So I back off and try to avoid them. This is very, very difficult to do. Richmond, the city where I live, is at least fifty to sixty per cent black. I only go out when it is necessary, like when I have a music gig. I have even been fired from volunteer work.

From the time I was six years old in 1940, through all of my hospital stays, and all the doctors I have seen and all the medications I have taken, Tourette was never mentioned. I was just told that I had a nervous condition or St. Vitus' Dance. I was even thought to have evil spirits! I took psychoanalysis for years with no results. I kept in touch with my doctor at Eastern State Hospital, and he was the one who informed me about Tourette. So from 1940 until sometime around 35 years later, I was misdiagnosed. My doctor told me about a medication that people with Tourette were using at that time.

It was called Haldol (that's the short name—I can't spell the long name). So I went to Medical College of Virginia, where I already had a medical record, and after a lot of red tape I was prescribed some Haldol. I remember being very much against it because I was told there were after-effects. I waited two weeks before I finally took it. I think they were 10 mg. pills, and I didn't know how long it would take. Nothing happened for a while—I was still having both vocal and motor tics. Then I became very restless and antsy. I could not keep still, I was always moving. I could not sit down; I could not sleep. It even interfered with my music—I could not keep my hands on my bass, and I could not concentrate at all. And the tics were as bad as ever. So I stopped taking Haldol, and the symptoms went away.

Over the years I have tried at least 25 other medications with no results. I am still seeing a psychiatrist and have been for 10 years. My tics wax and wane—sometimes I have control for a short while, and then it's *tic...tic...tic*. I have prayed for relief, but God has been silent in my life. But I have not lost my faith, and I won't.

As of now, I am 75 years old, and in good health. I still play music on a regular basis—that is also a gift from God. I am blessed in so many ways, but the gift of music is only second to the gift of life. Praise Him!

I don't know if a cure will be found in my lifetime, but maybe someone will benefit from this story, and what I have gone through for 75 years. What is it? ***It's Tourette—that's what makes me tic.***

Victor Mizelle

1206 West Franklin St.—Apt. 11
Richmond, VA 23220
804 303-6683

OBJECTIVE: A position in mail services or production

PROFILE: Dependable, responsible and cooperative team player

EMPLOYMENT BACKGROUND

1997-Present **Goodwill Industries, Inc.** – Richmond, VA
Production Worker – (Through AARP Employment
Program)
Sort, ticket and price incoming clothing for
distribution to the retail stores for resale. *(Quit because
of Tourette)*

1994-1997 **Virginia Commonwealth University** – Richmond, VA
Senior Grounds Worker
Maintained university parking lots in a clean and
orderly manner. *(Fired because of Tourette)*

1993-1994 **Virginia Employment Commission** – Richmond, VA
Postal Assistant
Prepared incoming and outbound business mail. Sorted
and delivered daily mail to all agency departments.
Maintained accurate postal records.

April 1992- **Pleasants Hardware** – Richmond, VA
October 1992 Warehouse Attendant
Responsible for stocking inventory in the warehouse
and on the sales floor. *(Fired because of Tourette)*

April 1991- **North American Marketing Corp.** – Richmond, VA
November 1991 Zipsort Material Handler
Pre-sorted mail by zip code, matched and collated mail
job orders. Handled incoming materials for stocking
and delivery. *(Fired because of Tourette)*

1986-1990 **Civitan Work Shop** – Richmond, VA
Material Handler

Operated shrink-wrap machines and electric scales. Assisted in
supervision of handicapped clients to complete work. *(Fired, was accused
of sexually touching one of the retarded clients—not true.)*

References Upon Request